CW00644491

POCKET
MANAGER

POCKET
MANAGER

*The essentials of
practical management
from A to Z*

THE ECONOMIST IN ASSOCIATION WITH
HAMISH HAMILTON LTD
Published by the Penguin Group
Penguin Books Ltd, 27 Wrights Lane, London W8 5TZ, England
Penguin Books USA Inc., 375 Hudson Street, New York,
New York 10014, USA
Penguin Books Australia Ltd, Ringwood, Victoria, Australia
Penguin Books Canada Ltd, 10 Alcorn Avenue, Toronto,
Ontario, Canada M4V 3B2
Penguin Books (NZ) Ltd, 182–190 Wairau Road, Auckland 10,
New Zealand

Penguin Books Ltd, Registered Offices:
Harmondsworth, Middlesex, England

First published by The Economist Books Ltd 1992
Second edition published by Hamish Hamilton Ltd
in association with The Economist Books Ltd 1994

1 3 5 7 9 10 8 6 4 2

Copyright © The Economist Newspaper Ltd, 1992, 1994

Chief contributor   Tim Hindle

Printed in Great Britain by the Bath Press

A CIP catalogue record for this book is available
from the British Library

ISBN 0-241-00237-0

CONTENTS

Introduction   vi

Part 1 Essays   **1**
Management in the 1990s   3
Human resources   8
The bottom line: what does it mean?   12
The key to the Japanese miracle   16
Terrified of IT?   21

Part 2 A–Z   **27**

Part 3 Appendixes   **221**
 1 The UK's most admired companies   223
 2 The USA's most admired companies   223
 3 The world's most productive industrial
       companies   223
 4 The world's most profitable industrial
       companies   224
 5 The world's biggest companies by
       industry   225
 6 Comparative corporate tax survey   226
 7 EC statutory retirement age   226
 8 EC public spending on R&D   226
 9 The most expensive cities in the world   227
10 Relative salaries around the world in
       terms of purchasing power   227
11 EC average weekly working hours   227
12 EC average days paid vacation   228
13 Comparative labour costs   228
14 Top 50 of *Fortune Global 500*, 1992   229

Glossary   **232**

Recommended reading list   **234**

INTRODUCTION

Pocket Manager is one in a new series of books that bring the clarity for which *The Economist* is famous to the often confusing subject of management.

It is written by Tim Hindle, a former management editor of *The Economist*, and is divided into three parts. Part 1 consists of essays which look at some of the issues that are likely to be at the top of managers' agendas in the 1990s.

Part 2 is an A–Z of the main terms that managers use in their everyday working life, but which they perhaps do not always feel that they fully understand. The A–Z also includes modern jargon words (like just-in-time and IT), and a sprinkling of those foreign words that are becoming part of the language of management, a language that is nevertheless even more firmly based in English than it ever was.

Throughout this section are a number of checklists to help managers in their daily business. The book is sprinkled with lively quotations from both managers and pundits. These help to show that management is a broad human endeavour with plenty of room for wit and creativity as well as for triumph and disappointment.

In this section words in small capitals usually indicate a separate entry, thus enabling readers to find other relevant information (though they should note that abbreviations such as IBM are also in small capitals).

Part 3 consists of appendixes with information in the form of tabulated data, together with a glossary and reading list.

The Pocket Management series is designed to take the mystique out of business jargon in a stimulating and entertaining way. Other titles in the series include:
Pocket Finance
Pocket MBA
Pocket Marketing
Pocket Negotiator
Pocket Strategy

Part 1

ESSAYS

Part I

Essays

MANAGEMENT IN THE 1990s

Managers have an identity problem. Everyone thinks they know what economists are and what they do. A manager can be a lot of things; or, some might say, not enough things. One problem is that management is a discipline that embraces a host of others – from computer sciences to law, from psychology to statistics. It has nothing that is unique to it; it is a sort of academic monster, made up from others' parts.

The enormous growth of MBA (Master of Business Administration) courses in recent years has had at least one unintended benefit: it has helped to identify the bundle of skills that constitutes management, and it has thus helped young managers feel that at least they know what they should know.

With the A-Z that is the core of the books in this series, the problem has been not to decide what to include, but to decide what to exclude. "There are few topics that can be regarded as completely useless to managers" begins one recent handbook on the subject. It then goes on to tell its readers in almost 600 pages about (among other things) the higher algebra of econometrics and the nature of colour blindness.

Focusing away from the blind side

We have narrowed our focus somewhat, and colour blindness falls outside it. We have decided to be influenced by the fact that management, like everything else, is subject to fashion. The emphasis given to different aspects of it depends on the ethos of the time.

In the 1980s that ethos was dominated by three things in particular.

1 Following the sun. There was a fascination in the USA and Europe with unlocking the secrets of the super-successful Japanese. These were seen to lie mostly in their methods of production; in minimising inventories and work-in-progress; and in introducing "quality management" at all levels of the organisation.

2 The metaphysics of maths. The numerate skills of the accountants and corporate planners who could seemingly create great wealth through takeovers without ever visiting a factory plant or a service point-of-sale.

3 Internationalisation. Driven by the "global" theories of Theodore Levitt at Harvard, by the extraordinarily rapid development of telecommunications and computers, by the increasing mobility of capital and by the harmonisation of consumer lifestyles across the developed world, the ability to think and act internationally became crucial. All of a sudden "cultural adaptability" and a second language became essential baggage for every ambitious manager.

For the 1990s we foresee three slightly different dominant features.

1 Internationalisation. This will undoubtedly continue to exert a strong influence on companies for years to come, and foreign investment is likely to outpace foreign trade as the main vehicle for it. Large companies will lose their national identities as managers work beside colleagues from a host of different nations, and the language of management (still largely English) will come to adopt more expressions from other languages.

2 Technology. There are still lessons for managers to learn from the military; from the 1991 Gulf War came the clear message that today's technology can provide overwhelming competitive advantage. The management of rapidly changing technology will be a key skill for the 1990s. In the service-dominated industries of North America and Western Europe that means information technology in particular.

3 Management of change. This is perhaps the biggest challenge for the 1990s. If there has been one discovery in recent years – by companies, their managers and those who advise them – it is the (perhaps blindingly obvious) fact that all things change. Markets change, the political and economic environment changes, and the science of management itself changes.

Future perfect: times of tension
This is not to say that all managers have until recently been assuming the opposite, but there has been an implicit assumption that things are changing, or being changed, in order to achieve some static state of perfection. The brave who would occasionally admit that such a state could never be reached would not deny that it existed.

Today that assumption is being abandoned. The rapidly increasing pace of change has brought home to managers the fact that they must live, to some extent, in a state of permanent chaos, a dynamic state that has already been identified by management gurus like Tom Peters. In this world, functions and lines of responsibility are left much less clearly defined.

Woman management
To understand what this change means we need to look back at the history of management, for management is at least as old as the first recorded housewife. Even if she was swathed in animal skins and used conch shells for currency, this primeval woman would have had a sense of budgeting and cost control. She would also have known a bit about organisation theory, having to choose when to dispatch one offspring to collect kindling and another to milk the goat.

In this pre-Toyota, pre-Toshiba era she would almost certainly have known a bit about "dynamic" concepts such as JIT (just-in-time). Her boiled beans and barbecued ribs had to be ready for her huntsman husband at the very moment when he lost the scent of one animal and before he caught the scent of another. She had neither the room nor the refrigeration to "time-shift" her beloved's meals.

Soldiering on
Somewhere along the line, however, management

became a male prerogative. The development of the science passed over to the military and to joyless empire builders, such as Alexander the Great, Hadrian, Genghis Khan and Napoleon. These men combined the skills of abstract strategy with those of practical logistics. But they thought in static terms. Military campaigns followed the book; and like every good book they had a beginning, a middle and an end.

The organisational structures needed for the military's finite campaigns were very different from those in the open-ended family around the first recorded housewife. They were authoritarian, with strict rules and hierarchies that sacrificed individual initiative for the benefits of a machine-like efficiency.

Operating by the book

The Industrial Revolution in Europe and North America grafted these skills on to those of the fifteenth century Italian book-keepers who had introduced quantitative measurement to the business of business. Factory workers were expected to perform like soldiers; they were given instructions and targets, with no scope to question them. Like soldiers, they were hired for little but their arms and legs.

New thoughts

To some degree the science of management since has been a continuing effort to break away from the precision and rigidity inherited from those (inevitably male) soldiers and accountants. A turning point came with the most famous industrial experiment of all time. Known as the Hawthorne Investigation, it started in 1927 at the Western Electric Company's Hawthorne factory in Chicago, and its most famous finding was that workers responded to changes in their physical environment (bright or dim lighting, for example) far less than they responded to the fact that somebody was thinking about their environment. It was the changing of the lighting itself that motivated them, not whether it was bright or dim.

National differences
Countries have moved at varying speeds from there. With its enthusiasm for new ideas, the USA embraced the thinking of the early industrial psychologists and their followers more enthusiastically than the UK. There the managerial mentality of retired army officers and administrators of empire was more difficult to shake off. Perhaps because they lost a war, Japanese and German managers found it easier to reject the military model, without at the same time allowing themselves to be led down every new blind alley like in fad-conscious America.

Squaring the circle
In any case, the static industrial model of military cohorts neatly arranged for the occasional foray and immediate regrouping is now obsolete everywhere. In today's society of knowledge-workers, management is finding that it has come full circle, that it has more in common with the primeval housewife than it has with Napoleon on the battlefield. At least that should give women better opportunities in the future; it will certainly emphasise the softer sides of the art – skill and style – at the expense of strategy and structure.

HUMAN RESOURCES

In the 1980s a wide range of companies finally came to believe the old adage about their most valuable resources being their human resources. For many of the decade's fast-growing service companies they were virtually their only resource. Advertising agencies and consultancies would joke nervously about how all their assets came in and out of the front door every day.

People make a difference

With this upgrading of human resources came an upgrading of the personnel function. For many years the personnel department had been a corporate cul-de-sac into which were shunted men and women who had risen above their level of competence. It was often a no-exit career move. With the new-found status of human resources that has changed, however, and with the change has come a new name for the personnel job: human-resource management.

This improvement in status has been somewhat uneven across Europe. In early 1990 Price Waterhouse, an international firm of accountants and consultants, and the Cranfield School of Management carried out a pan-European survey of human-resource management.

One of their findings was the extent to which the head of personnel had a seat on the board in different countries.

	%
Sweden	87
France	84
Spain	78
UK	63
Germany (West)	19

The German figure looks strange, but it is not inconsistent with another of the study's findings – that Germany has the largest percentage of companies (13%) where the head of personnel is never consulted about corporate strategy.

So, too, does the management of them

Another question in the Price Waterhouse/Cranfield survey tried to find out which skills companies reckoned they would need most in the early 1990s. Comfortably top of the list in almost every country (Spain was a notable exception) came "people-management skills", such as the ability to motivate and to get people to work well in teams. Computers and technology came second.

Complicated spirits . . .

Motivation is at the heart of human-resource management, and it is a complex beast. One of the lessons that the increasingly powerful human-resource managers learnt in the 1980s was that if they spent long hours devising clever pay scales and infinitely subtle bonus schemes they were largely wasting their time. Money alone could not motivate the right people to stay and to perform better.

Yet for much of the 1980s money was embedding itself more deeply into the reward system. "Performance-related bonus schemes" proliferated. On one calculation, in 1980 only about 10% of British companies offered executive bonus schemes. Ten years later less than 10% did not offer them. They became so much a part of pay packages that one consultant referred to them as "salary in drag".

Nobody, however, could find a link between corporate performance and the level (or indeed the existence) of such schemes. Some of the highest bonuses were going to managers of the worst companies, and vice versa. The Japanese were able to ridicule American managers for the size of their rewards and for the almost inverse relationship between them and performance.

There were studies suggesting that employees who claimed that financial issues were at the root of their discontent were usually hiding a deeper unhappiness with more abstract elements of their working life. It is easier to go to a "boss" and say, "You are not paying me enough. I'm leaving", than it is to go and say, "This job does not make me feel proud of myself. I'm leaving". All this put a large question mark over pay as the main motivator behind successful companies.

... must be understood by their priorities ...

Awareness of such complexity has made the human-resource specialists look back to the 1960s, when the work of men like Abraham Maslow defined a framework for thinking about the psychology of the workplace. Maslow looked at the things that an individual needs as either physiological (like oxygen and water) or psychological (like security and recognition).

These needs come in a definite order of priority, ranked by the length of time that people can do without them. For the physiological needs the order is (from shortest to longest): oxygen, water, food, rest, constant body temperature and reproduction. The psychological needs Maslow also ranked from shortest to longest: security/self-control, social relationships, self-esteem, status/recognition, achievement/challenge, power, creativity and self-actualisation.

Early items on the list take priority over later ones. So somebody gasping for oxygen is not going to be too concerned about making babies, for example. Likewise, people with no job security (a word whose stem means "without fear") are not going to worry about getting on well with their colleagues at work until they do feel secure. In other words, the firm that hires and fires willy-nilly cannot expect good teamwork.

... and not isolated by machines

This is rather different from the working environment envisaged by management soothsayers a short time ago. A combination of demographic change and new technology was supposed to distance people from each other. In the post-robotic age motivation and human relationships would count for little. People would no longer work in a huddle on production lines. They would be freed by machines to become "knowledge-workers", better educated and better trained. The prime relationship of these knowledge-workers would be with machines – the computer and the telephone – and these would formalise and filter messages between them. People would work independently, from homes deep in the countryside, telecommuting with other workers also deep in the countryside.

In recent years many companies in Europe and the USA did shrink their workforces dramatically. Not because demographics had created a labour shortage; but because they went to the corporate health farm and there shed some excess fat. But their slimmed-down workforces did not disappear into the solitude of sylvan cottages. To many people's surprise, information technology and robotics increased rather than diminished the value of human contact between workers freed from the mind-numbing tasks that technology had taken over. The independent telecommuters, to whom many tasks that had once been done in-house were being subcontracted, preferred to stay close to corporate headquarters. The need for social relationships among the new-style knowledge-workers increased. In Maslow's scheme of things that had to be at the expense of creativity and achievement.

THE BOTTOM LINE: WHAT DOES IT MEAN?

Frederick Herzberg, a distinguished American professor of management, wrote:

> *Our love affair with numbers is the root cause of the passionlessness of the 1980s. We try to escape the nihilism of zero by putting our dreams and emotions into greater and greater numbers. How many pieces of information will fit on a computer chip? How many billions can we add or cut from the budget? Numbers numb our feelings for what is being counted and lead to adoration of the economies of scale. Passion is in feeling the quality of experience, not in trying to measure it.*

Mr Herzberg eloquently represents today's counter-reaction to the authority of the accountants and the number-crunchers who dominated the 1980s. That domination was particularly strong in the USA and in the UK where a whole generation of top managers had been first trained as accountants. (After the second world war accountancy had been seen as a substitute for a then non-existent management education.) Senior executives of the 1980s could read a set of accounts very easily. They had been led to believe that accounts could record precisely the profits of a company, in the same way that they could record precisely the number of widgets coming off the production line; but they could have been led to believe exactly the opposite. Accountants are frequently undecided about the best way to measure things other than widgets. They disguise their doubts by issuing so-called accounting standards on contentious issues like goodwill, extraordinary items or deferred tax. These standards attempt to dispel the ambiguity that rigorous accountants find uncomfortable.

Bubble trouble
Inflation accounting was the one issue that might

have alerted businessmen and financiers to the fact that accounts should not be taken too literally. In the late 1970s, when inflation was well into double figures in many developed countries, accountants spent hours tussling with the question of how to cope with it in accounts. There was no doubt that they had a problem. Something which cost $100 at the beginning of a year was costing, say, $115 by the end of the year. Mixing nominal values on January 1st with nominal values on December 31st was like adding inches and centimetres.

All sorts of different ways of handling this problem were suggested, and eventually accountants settled for one of them. Large companies were instructed to publish inflation-adjusted statements for a three-year experimental period. By 1983, the end of the three years, inflation was way down in single figures, and to their great relief companies were allowed quietly to drop the awkward attempt to take account of changing prices. A precise and unique measurement of profit in a time of inflation had proved to be illusory.

Brand balancing

There were other signs that the emperor of accounting precision was wearing no clothes. For example, the popular new accounting pastime in the late 1980s of valuing "brand names" (intangible assets like the name Smirnoff or Kit-Kat) threw up some extraordinary nonsense. Accountants decided that the value of newly-purchased brands could be added to the balance sheet, but not the value of those that had been developed in-house over a number of years. So Smirnoff (plus a few other lesser names bought by Grand Metropolitan in 1987) became worth $500m, while Gordon's Gin, for example, was not officially worth a penny.

One world, different rules

Another sign came as the European Community increasingly attempted to harmonise accounting rules throughout its member states. It became apparent that there were wide and irreconcilable differences between UK practice and that of many continental countries. In general the differences tended to increase the profits of UK companies vis-à-vis those on the continent. There are three good examples of this.

1   Cost of sales. There are two basic methods of measuring this – FIFO (first in, first out) and LIFO (last in, first out). If the prices of inputs are constant LIFO and FIFO give the same results, but in the real world (where there is inflation) FIFO produces higher profits for a given level of sales than LIFO. British companies must use FIFO.

2   Stocks. These can be valued either at cost or at realisable value. If they are valued at cost then their worth is understated in the balance sheet (assuming that they will eventually be sold for more than their cost – a perfectly valid assumption for most companies' stocks). Writing up their value raises the cost of stocks taken into the next year's profit and loss account, and so lowers profit. British companies normally value stock at cost.

3   Depreciation. There are big differences in the treatment of depreciation, and to some extent companies can choose what rate at which to depreciate their assets. The higher the depreciation, the lower the profit. In general UK companies set aside less through depreciation (and through other discretionary provisions) than companies on the continent.

Termism – a question of attitudes
US and UK companies are tempted to make all the little (and sometimes not so little) accounting tweaks that they can to increase reported profits because they are under the constant scrutiny of the stockmarket, which will hammer ruthlessly any downward kink in the corporate growth curve, or any cut in a company's dividend. On the continent companies' shares are less widely

held, and so they worry less about the stockmarket. They try to smooth out the good years with the bad by sometimes using accounting techniques actually to reduce reported profits.

So accounts are not a clear, precise snapshot of anything. They are more like a picture of the surface of some faraway planet – interesting, but in need of interpretation. Some might see a mountain where others see a crater.

Profit motives

If accounts are imprecise, then so too are measures of profit. Is that something to worry about? Yes if you think that profit is the only measure of corporate virility, but no if you take the view of people like the management writer Charles Handy. He believes that companies are not on this earth primarily to make profits. When he was an expatriate manager with an oil company Mr Handy found the slogan that had been above the blackboard in every classroom at his business school – "The purpose of a company is to maximise medium-term earnings (that is profits) per share" – to be "very remote, very long-term, very intellectual, very unreal". It was no use to him either as a measure of his performance or as a guide to his future behaviour.

He came to believe that profits were useful merely to do things or to make things more abundantly and better. They have a role as a necessary condition for continuing to do business; but they are not sufficient, and they never will be.

THE KEY TO THE JAPANESE MIRACLE

Western managers have developed an inferiority complex about the Japanese. It has come from being told again and again that whatever a western company does, the Japanese are sure to have done, to be doing, or to be about to do it better. Despite occasional books and articles telling us, comfortingly, that there is still corporate excellence in the West, or that the sun will also set on Japan, the complex has deepened as the Japanese have progressed from one triumph to another.

Japan's secret seven
It became a popular pastime in the 1980s for western gurus to try to distil Japan's business "secret" into seven easy pieces. It all lay in their attitude to the Seven Ss, said one popular management book. The Ss were strategy, structure, systems, staff, style, skills and superordinate goals, a fairly comprehensive list that seems sure to have trawled the answer somewhere. More targeted explanations have also been plentiful. Here are ten – most of them containing a grain of truth, none of them providing a complete answer.

1 Rip-off one. "The Japanese are copycats. They pinch the brilliant ideas of western Nobel prize-winners and turn them into gadgets that people want to buy." True, the Japanese have failed to star in the Nobel lists, but remember that the prizes are awarded by western judges who value "pure" science above the practical application of science in which the Japanese excel.

It was Japan's Sony that did much of the early research on the VCR (video cassette recorder). Sony's system was then virtually wiped off the commercial map by its Japanese rival Matsushita, a company notorious for starting late and overtaking early. Both Sony and Matsushita spend more on R&D as a percentage of sales than any of their rivals in the West.

2 Rip-off two. "Not only do the Japanese copy technical ideas, they copy management ideas too." Look at the recent book, Makers of Management, a history of "men and women who have changed the business world". It includes only one Japanese, Kenichi Ohmae, and he is an Americanised McKinsey-trained consultant.

Even what seem like Japanese ideas are really foreign transplants. Quality management came from the teaching of the American W. Edwards Deming, after whom the Japanese have respectfully named a prestigious business award. The commonsense idea of just-in-time (JIT) was also scarcely original, although the Japanese application of it certainly was.

3 Shinto rules. "It's all to do with their religion; it teaches them to be resigned to their lot." There is indeed a great difference between the fatalistic Shinto faith and the individualistic Judaic-Christian tradition of the West. For example, the Japanese go to great lengths to avoid causing others to lose face; the ambitious westerner will often go to great lengths to ensure somebody else does lose face. That makes a big difference in business. The Japanese feel secure in the knowledge that they will not be embarrassed by their colleagues or their boss.

4 Educating Edo. "It's because they have no business schools and no MBAs." This is the half-humorous jibe of western businessmen disillusioned with their intake of overeducated and underexperienced Masters in Business Administration. While the Japanese may not have formal business schools, they do have plenty of on-the-job training. An American has said that the Japanese have just one business school, and it is called the USA.

5 It's not cricket. "They are protectionist and compete unfairly." Until 1967 this was undoubtedly true. Barriers to trade and government restrictions on foreign investment reinforced

Japan's natural aversion to things foreign. Western firms were indifferent to this protectionism for as long as Japan's economy remained insignificant. Then they kicked up a fuss, and many of the barriers came down.

By then Japan was no longer the cheap-labour base that many of the potential foreign investors were looking for; importers had to compete with well-established local firms in a labyrinthine distribution system that only locals fully understood. Nowadays it is debatable whether Japan's remaining barriers to trade and investment are more onerous than anybody else's.

6 Investing in the future. "Japanese companies invest more in plant and equipment, so their factories are more productive." This has certainly been true over most of the past 30 years. But it may not be primarily because of the availability of capital, or of technology. It may be more because Japanese workers, secure in their lifetime employment, do not feel threatened by new technology. On the contrary, they welcome it because any improvement in profits also improves their traditional (and variable) profit-related bonus.

7 Saving it. "They squirrel away all their money while the rest of the world has a good time." Savings rates in Japan (like investment rates) are usually higher than in other industrialised countries, but who is having the good time? The American with the large house, uncertain income and huge mortgage; or the Japanese with the small flat, secure job and money in the bank?

8 Slave labour. "Japanese workers are treated like slaves." If so, then never were slaves so productive. By 1980 Matsushita's sales per employee were double those of Siemens or Philips. The slave argument rests on the cramped living conditions of most Japanese families, and the docile way in which workers will agree to shift to new jobs or new districts. The cramped living conditions are determined by the small habitable area of the Japanese islands, not by Japanese employers, and who but a slave would not choose to change jobs and workplace several times during his or her life?

9 Long-termism. "Japanese companies do not have to bother about making profits, because they are buttressed by the notorious *zaibatsu* industrial and financial conglomerates." All they care about is market share, and about stealing it from others. (By the way, Matsushita, whose focus on market share is notorious, is not a member of any *zaibatsu*.)

In general Japanese companies' financial relationships are quite different from those in the West. Relationships with banks are long-term and supportive, not short-term and confrontational. Moreover, the shareholder is not king. Keeping them happy with a constantly rising stream of dividends is not a high priority. Shareholders have to look to growth and capital gains for their return.

10 Genes power. "The Japanese have some sort of genetically superior business ability, a bit like the Jews, and are plotting to use it to gain revenge for losing the war." "Jap zips zap Brits" ran the famous headline when YKK opened a factory in the UK in 1972.

This is racist nonsense that is false in practice (Honda executives swear they had no other purpose when entering the US market than to try to sell something to the Americans); and false in theory. Japan knows perfectly well that it depends for its survival on selling goods in non-Japanese markets. Only by ensuring that those markets grow can it grow itself.

Feet in the ground

There is nothing extra-terrestrial about Japanese business; it uses the same factors of production as anybody else – capital, land and labour. It has little land, and after the war it had even less capital.

The task of rebuilding the Japanese economy fell squarely upon Japanese workers, and they have made a remarkably fine job of it. Their achievement rests on the following basis: a good education and training; a culturally ingrained attention to detail (the Japanese are "fussy"); and a vision of themselves as valuable members of an industrial society, not wage-slaves straining always to be free to do their own thing.

TERRIFIED OF IT?

It took a long time for the machinery of information technology – computers and advanced telecommunications – to reach into the offices of senior and middle managers. Now that they have arrived, however, they have already started revolutionising the way that companies work.

Rising from the depths

Computers crept into the corporation gradually. At first, huge mainframes were shut up in vast dingy basements, whirring away at night and supervised by a pallid breed of night-watchman called a computer manager.

Unlike humans, computers grew smaller as they grew up. As they shrank they moved upstairs from the basement and into different departments – finance, stock control, etc. They moved first to departments where their expense could most easily be justified in terms of the manpower that IT saved. Only in government organisations, like census departments and tax authorities, where monumental tasks of paper-processing were threatening to strangle them into irreversible coma, were they accepted more widely and more quickly.

On to the factory floor

In time, with the development of robotics, computers moved on to the factory floor. Fiat, the Italian car manufacturer, saw extensive use of robots as the only way for European manufacturers to compete with the Japanese. They would reduce to a minimum the need for Italian labour, whose expectations were so far above those of Japanese workers that they could not hope to produce competitively priced products.

Slowly to the top

This piecemeal development left companies with a number of "islands" of IT in far-flung areas such as design, accounting and manufacturing. Senior managers who could not justify IT for themselves on any normal cost-benefit analysis were left at sea amid the islands. A 1988 survey by the Massachusetts Institute of Technology (MIT) estimated that no more than 10-15% of senior executives in large American companies had computers on their desks, and no more than half of them were using their computers properly.

Since then visual display units (VDUS) have gradually come closer to the chief executive's desk for a number of reasons.

1 They started to be more "executive friendly". Led by Apple, computer manufacturers developed a range of machines that avoided the trauma of sending the over-50s off for typing lessons.

2 A common phenomenon of the 1980s – the streamlining of company headquarters – left executives with fewer support staff. They saw computers as a possible replacement for that disappearing support.

3 They also saw that the economic world around them was changing unmanageably fast. There was no longer any permanence to interest or exchange rates; new products came and went as quickly as the seasons. There was no way that they could keep up-to-date with the impact these changes were having on their businesses if they continued to use old-style paper-based reporting systems. As a "pre-tech exec", the boss of Rank Xerox used to receive regular reports the size of telephone directories. After he took to the computer these were whittled down to five on-screen pages.

Linking up
Once the corporate sea was filled with islands of IT, companies wanted to bring the islands together into a single unit. Telecommunications then came into its own, linking computers in one part of the organisation with computers in another. This "networking" allowed all parts of the organisation (at home and abroad) to have access to

huge amounts of information that they had never before imagined would be available to them.

Naturally this made senior managers nervous. They understood as well as any petty potentate in the Dark Ages that information is power. And was not power their exclusive monopoly?

Opening up . . .

They became even more nervous when they let themselves think about the future of telecommunications. They were being told that the development of fibre optics was going to cause an explosion in telecommunications capacity. Arthur Andersen, the leading consultant in IT, prophesied that before the end of the 1990s 10m conversations would be carried simultaneously by a single fibre optic, compared with 3,000 in the late 1980s. That should definitely do something dramatic to the price of telecommunications. It should also destroy one of the main arguments for not disseminating information more widely throughout companies. "We are moving towards the capability to communicate anything to anyone, anywhere, by any form – voice, data, text or image – at the speed of light," predicted John Naisbett and Patricia Aburdene in their bestseller, *Megatrends 2000*.

The future capability of telecommunications threatens to change the function of management in the corporation of the future. For a start, its job will no longer be one of deciding which information to filter to which department. All information will be available to everybody. The manager's task will be to make it meaningful, and then to act accordingly. This does not imply that companies will need fewer managers, rather that they will need better-trained managers – better trained to understand what the messages that they are receiving about their external environment (and about their company) are trying to tell them.

. . . and informating

An expression has arisen to describe this new phenomenon: IT is not "automating" management;

it is, rather, "informating" it. Automating makes humans redundant; informating makes them even more valuable.

Shoshana Zuboff, a professor of business administration at Harvard, is a leading proponent of the theory of the "informated" as opposed to the "automated" company. In one interview she described clearly what she believes is involved in this process:

Throughout history technology has been designed to substitute for the human body and do the same things only faster, with less or no human intervention, at lower cost. Over the past few decades this logic has come to be known as automation. The assumption is that more automation means higher productivity. The more technology you have, the fewer people you need. . . In my research, however, I observed that these rules about automation did not hold true for information technology. The introduction of computer technology did not necessarily mean you could get by with fewer, less intelligent people. With a technology that informates, you start to have masses and masses of data that hold all the riches, all the opportunities to learn something about the business that never could have been learned before. The business and its various dynamics become transparent, and this transparency is the new source of wealth of the company.

This brings us to the second meaning of informating. It is about the strategic intent of the firm, and implies a profoundly different conception of organisation and management. Informating represents the changing distribution of knowledge, authority and power. It means that the new purpose and function of management is the fusing of work and learning. Unfortunately, under the automation paradigm the people on the front lines are not trained to understand information or to do anything with it. Control of most information still rests in upper management's hands.

Stimulating stuff, which in essence seems to say that managers should not be afraid of IT. It will not automate their jobs away. In fact it will do quite the opposite: it should informate them to new heights of fulfilment.

Part 2

A–Z

ABOVE-THE-LINE

An accounting term referring to certain items in the PROFIT AND LOSS ACCOUNT. These are items that appear above the net PROFIT "line" in the line-by-line P&L statement. The net profit figure is arrived at by subtracting the ordinary expenses of running the business from the ordinary revenues of the business. Any extraordinary revenues or expenses are supposed to appear BELOW-THE-LINE.

Net profit is a key indicator of corporate performance, so there is an extraordinary temptation for companies to confuse the ordinary with the extraordinary. Net profit can be made to look better by putting as many expenses as possible below-the-line, and as much revenue as possible above it. ACCOUNTING STANDARDS on extraordinary items try to fix where this mobile line should be.

ACCEPTANCE CREDIT

A BILL OF EXCHANGE that has been endorsed by a bank; that is, the bank has given its guarantee that the bill will be paid. This is a popular way of financing trade between buyers and sellers who do not know each other, but who do trust each other's bank. The bank charges a fee for its endorsement. Sellers who have a bill "accepted" by a reputable bank can then sell the bill (at a DISCOUNT) and get immediate payment for the goods they have sold.

ACCOUNTING STANDARDS

When accountants are uncertain about how to VALUE particular items in companies' accounts, their professional associations get together to rule on what they consider to be "best practice". This advice they issue in the form of accounting standards. Particularly controversial areas that the associations have tried to rule on include accounting for INFLATION, for foreign-currency conversion, for deferred tax and for GOODWILL.

Different countries give their standards different weight. In Canada they have legal backing; in the USA they are compulsory for companies registered with the SECURITIES AND EXCHANGE COMMISSION; and in the UK they are voluntary. Any company not following them has to explain why.

ACCOUNTS

The records of a COMPANY's transactions. The traditional method of keeping accounts is the DOUBLE-ENTRY system in which debits are entered on the left-hand side of the "ledger" (the book of accounts), and credits on the right-hand side. For every debit there is an equal and opposite credit.

Accounts also come in several variations of this basic model as follows.

- **Annual accounts.** The PROFIT AND LOSS ACCOUNT, the BALANCE SHEET, plus any other financial statements required by law. These have to be presented by companies to their shareholders as a record of the companies' performance during their FINANCIAL YEAR.
- **Consolidated accounts.**
- **Interim accounts.** Accounts produced by companies covering a period that is less than a full financial year.
- **Nominal accounts.** The book of accounts for everyday expenses, like salaries and post.
- **Personal accounts.** In olden days, the only book of accounts; the one that recorded who was owed money by the company and who owed money to the company.
- **Real accounts.** The book of accounts for "real" things, that is things that you can touch, like buildings and machinery.

Accounts are a snapshot of a business at a moment in time. Take a picture the following day and the scene may look very different. As with many of us, companies like to look their best when they are photographed, and sometimes dress for the occasion.
M.A. Pitcher

*An accountant is a man who puts his head in the
past and backs his ass into the future.*
Ross Johnson, ex-CEO, RJR Nabisco, from *Barbarians at
the Gate.*

ACCOUNTS PAYABLE
See CREDITOR.

ACCOUNTS RECEIVABLE
See DEBTOR.

ACID TEST
Also known as the "quick ratio", this is the ratio
of a COMPANY's LIQUID ASSETS (like cash, bank
balances and easily saleable SECURITIES) to its
short-term debts, that is, the money it owes
other people in the not-too-distant future. It is
widely used by financial analysts and bankers to
determine whether a company has sufficient
LIQUIDITY.

ACQUISITION
The purchase of a controlling interest in one COM-
PANY by another; popularly linked with mergers
through the expression M&A (short for mergers
and acquisitions). Acquisitions can be friendly
(when both companies agree to the purchase) or
hostile (when some shareholders sell out to the
buyer against the wishes of MANAGEMENT and
other shareholders). Whatever form they take,
acquisitions are rarely without pain for the acquir-
er and the acquired.

ADDED VALUE
Or "VALUE added", the difference between what a
COMPANY spends buying materials from outside,
and what it receives from selling its products. Out
of this added value the firm has to pay wages,
rent and interest. The rest is PROFIT.

Calculating the added value at different stages
of the production process can help a company
to identify the most profitable parts of its business.
It may show that certain processes would be

cheaper bought in from outside. In the COMPUTER and textile industries, for example, semi-finished products are shipped halfway across the world (and then back again) for LABOUR-intensive processes to be carried out in places where labour is cheap.

ADMINISTRATION

A UK corporate condition halfway between normal trading and bankruptcy; a version of the USA's CHAPTER 11. Administration was designed to free troubled companies from the claims and writs of creditors while they get their affairs in order.

The directors of a troubled COMPANY (or its creditors) ask the courts to appoint an "administrator" – normally an accountant – to run the company while it pursues an agreed rescue plan. The administrator is given a certain length of time (usually a matter of months) to effect the rescue plan and to gain the creditors' approval for it. Almost inevitably, creditors are asked to write off part of their debts in order to get some of them repaid.

In the case of a big PUBLIC COMPANY administration can (like Chapter 11) be very long, very expensive and, in the end, very unsatisfactory for creditors and shareholders.

ADVERTISING

The glamorous part of MARKETING in which a firm's products and services are fulsomely described in newspaper announcements, billboards, or in short films shown on television. The heart of the advertising industry is on Madison Avenue in New York. It passed briefly to London in the 1980s.

Advertising aims to inform consumers about products. It may also entertain them in the process. The only guarantee that it is not misleading is the advertising industry's own sanctions against its members.

David Ogilvy (founder of the Ogilvy & Mather advertising agency, now part of the WPP Group) once gave 16 tips on television advertising. They are hard to beat.

- [ ] Identify the brand and make it memorable: use its name within the first ten seconds; then play word games with it, or spell it out.
- [ ] Show the product and its packaging.
- [ ] If advertising food, show it in motion. Pour syrup over pancakes. Do not let it just sit there.
- [ ] Use close-ups.
- [ ] Start with a bang. If you only finish with a bang your audience will not see it. They will be busy boiling a kettle.
- [ ] If you do not have much to say, put it in song; but make sure audiences can understand the words of your jingle.
- [ ] Sound effects can be very powerful; bacon sizzling, or coffee percolating, for example.
- [ ] Try to have actors talking on camera, rather than voice-overs.
- [ ] Reinforce your message by superimposing it in type as the soundtrack speaks the words.
- [ ] Avoid the visually banal; the happy family at the breakfast table, for example.
- [ ] Do not change scenes too often. Too many changes can be very confusing.
- [ ] Use a mnemonic, a visual device that is repeated again and again, like MGM's roaring lion.
- [ ] Show the product in use: the car on the road, or the beer being drunk.
- [ ] Do not forget that anything is possible on TV. Let your imagination rip.
- [ ] Make sure that advertisements are crystal clear. (David Ogilvy claimed that more than half the commercials he saw were incomprehensible.)
- [ ] Television commercials are very expensive. There is no research to prove it, but Ogilvy suspected that there is a negative correlation between the money spent on producing a television advertisement and its ability to sell a product.

AFFILIATE

A COMPANY, X, which is partly owned by another
company, Y, is said to be an affiliate of Y and of
all Y's other affiliates. Because of their relationship, affiliates' dealings with each other are not
always ARM'S LENGTH commercial transactions.

The word "affiliate" can also refer to non-
corporate entities that have close links. For example, individual TRADE UNIONS are "affiliated" to
their central organisation.

(See also ASSOCIATED COMPANY, SUBSIDIARY.)

AGENT

A central figure in most businesses, the agent is a
COMPANY or individual who has the authority to
carry out transactions with third parties on behalf
of somebody else (called "the principal"). Agents
are frequently used to buy or sell goods in
remote or inaccessible markets.

• **Sole agent.** Somebody with an exclusive
agreement to be the only person (or company)
allowed to buy or sell on behalf of the principal
in a particular geographic region.
• **Commission agent.** An agent who is reward-
ed by a commission; that is, an agreed percentage
of the VALUE of the goods that he or she buys or
sells.

In one sense managers are "agents" of a company's shareholders. Some see the shortcomings
of this agency relationship as one of the central
failings of capitalism.

AGM

See ANNUAL GENERAL MEETING.

ALLIANCE

The joining together of two corporations (often
competitors) in a loose link for what they see as
being their mutual benefit. Thus AT&T, the US
telecommunications company, and Olivetti, the
Italian computer company, formed an alliance
which involved AT&T in buying 25% of Olivetti,

and both sides promising to develop a lot of new business together in the fast-growing field of INFORMATION TECHNOLOGY. However, the alliance proved disappointing to both sides and AT&T has sold its stake. Undaunted, however, AT&T has formed at least half a dozen other strategic alliances with computer and telecommunications companies in Europe and Japan.

AMORTISATION
See DEPRECIATION.

ANALYST
In general, a person who is employed to analyse something or other. Nowadays two types of analyst feature strongly in the life of the corporation.

• **The systems analyst.** These are the people responsible for designing, installing and operating corporate COMPUTER systems. In the early days of the computer they were a breed apart. They spoke a language more obscure than the white-coated R&D technicians, and they had an arrogance that came from having the power to hold the whole corporation to ransom. As computers have grown smaller, and managers more familiar with them, the awesome power of the systems analyst has declined.

• **The investment analyst.** These are the bright young sparks in stockbroking firms who demand information about public companies from their managers, churn it about, and then show MANAGEMENT what a lousy job it is doing. A number of companies find that being answerable to investment analysts is one of the most onerous duties of being a PUBLIC COMPANY.

ANNUAL GENERAL MEETING
The gathering of shareholders that most companies are legally obliged to hold once a year. The annual general meeting (AGM) provides a rare opportunity for shareholders to meet and question those who run their COMPANY for them (the MANAGEMENT). In practice AGMs are usually tame

affairs. Everybody tries hard to avoid giving offence; shareholders agree to the dividend payment and to the reappointment of the auditors; and then everybody heads for the alcohol and cocktail sausages. If the COMPANY makes CONSUMER goods, then shareholders will expect to take a few of them home at the end of the day.

On the rare occasions when AGMs become lively it is because the company has been targeted by an active pressure group. For many years Barclays Bank's AGM was frequented by vocal anti-apartheid groups because of the bank's considerable investment in South Africa. The CONGLOMERATE Hanson found its AGM disturbed by Navajo Indians objecting to the pillage of their lands (as they saw it) by Peabody Coal, the USA's biggest coal-mining company and a subsidiary of Hanson.

If shareholders do not take AGMs seriously then top management becomes answerable to nobody but itself. Shareholders should not then be surprised to find themselves financing fleets of cars and jets and the building of self-aggrandising glass palaces called "headquarters".

ANNUAL REPORT
The official document sent to a COMPANY's shareholders telling them about the company's activities in the previous year. In general the report must, by law, contain certain things.

• An audited copy of the BALANCE SHEET and PROFIT AND LOSS ACCOUNT.
• The auditors' report on the ACCOUNTS.
• The DIRECTORS' report on the past year's performance.
• Consolidated accounts where the company owns a SUBSIDIARY.

Other information is often provided voluntarily.

• The chairman's report, a not always unintentionally vague statement of where the company is hoping to go.

- A CASH-FLOW statement which records MCI (money coming in) and MGO (money going out).
- A geographical and sectoral breakdown showing where turnover and PROFIT came from.
- A table of the company's five- or ten-year track record.

Many large companies would like to turn their annual reports into coffee-table books. As a rule, the less information provided, the more colourful and thick the report. The 1989 report of Guinness, the brewing company, contained a list of the names of 14 photographers who had worked on the report. That could stand in the company's own Book of Records.

Annual reports are not to be taken at face VALUE (see WINDOW-DRESSING). Their main value should lie in provoking awkward questions at the AGM and elsewhere.

Management is like taking a bath. First you wash yourself. Then second, you think. The problem with managers today is that too many are taking showers.
Antoine Riboud, head of BSN, the large French food group

ANNUALISED PERCENTAGE RATE

Often abbreviated to APR, a standard way of expressing the rate of interest on any form of credit. It is the rate that a flow of interest payments would represent if they were all paid as a single annual payment. The formula is:

$$\text{APR} = \frac{100 \times (1 + \text{rate})^n - 100}{(100)}$$

where n is the number of payments per year.

It is often a legal requirement that all loans offered to the general public show their APR. This is to frustrate loan sharks who want to advertise a rate of interest of "only 10%", when what they mean is 10% a month.

APPRAISAL

A systematic way of assessing the performance of employees. Until recently appraisal schemes were part of the process of deciding on promotions, pay rises or training needs. They only occurred at times of discrete change in an employee's career.

With the popularity of performance-related pay, appraisal schemes have become more like an integral part of everyday decisions about pay itself. Typically they consist of an annual interview with a senior manager. At the interview targets are set against which future performance can be measured.

Here are some points the appraiser should remember.

❒ Be prepared: give advance notice; allow adequate time; and ensure privacy.
❒ It is a two-way process.
❒ Review performance not personality.
❒ Ask open questions.
❒ Listen to the answers.
❒ Review the past and plan the future.
❒ Agree development needs and actions to be taken as a result.
❒ Encourage open, honest discussion.

APPRENTICESHIP

The period served by an apprentice; that is, somebody who signs a CONTRACT with an employer to work for a given period of time (usually for a nominal wage) in return for which the employer agrees to train the apprentice in a particular skill. The professions (medicine, accountancy and the law) used to have apprenticeship systems, but new recruits into these professions today generally arrive fully fledged, expecting to be fully paid.

Germany has a highly-developed apprenticeship system. Some 40% of all young people there receive vocational TRAINING. This combines part-time work with classroom education at special state-run vocational training centres. It is one reason for the high number of Germans with technology and engineering qualifications, and for the high quality of German technology.

APR
See ANNUALISED PERCENTAGE RATE.

ARBITRATION
An alternative procedure to the courts for settling commercial disputes. Those in dispute (over, say, the terms of a CONTRACT) turn to an independent third party whose judgment they have agreed, in advance, to accept should a dispute arise. The third party (the arbitrator) may be a panel of experts, in which case one of them will be appointed to make the final decision. An arbitrator's judgment is known as an "award".

Several international bodies (including the GATT and some international industry associations) have set up arbitration systems to help settle international commercial disputes.

There are a number of advantages to arbitration.

• Going through the courts can be long drawn-out and expensive, especially when it involves more than one jurisdiction.
• The parties to the dispute can choose as arbitrator someone who not only knows the law but who also knows their own specialist business.
• The process can take place in secret, which is valuable when companies are arguing about commercially sensitive matters.
• The venue and timing of the process is much more flexible than it is with a judge and his or her court attendants.
• Even when committed to arbitration, the parties involved do not necessarily give up their right subsequently to take the case to court.

A

ARM'S LENGTH

A transaction is said to be done "at arm's length" if it is carried out between a totally unrelated buyer and seller. If the buyer and seller are in some way related (first cousins, or a holding COMPANY and its SUBSIDIARY) then the price they agree between them might be affected by factors that would not apply in a totally free market.

Tax authorities hunt keenly to see that transactions between related companies are carried out at arm's length. Otherwise, by means of TRANSFER PRICING, large groups can easily avoid paying large amounts of tax.

ASSEMBLY LINE

In its time, a revolutionary system of manufacturing in which the product comes to the worker, instead of the worker coming to the product. An article moves along a line of workers, each of whom (called a "station") adds their bit of assembly before it passes on to the next worker. Ultimately the finished product drops off the end of the line.

One problem with assembly-line production is that unless each station's task takes exactly the same amount of time, the process is inefficient. Workers can be left idle while a process is completed further up the line. This problem can be overcome by using robots programmed to take exactly the same amount of time over each assembly-line task.

ASSESSMENT CENTRE

More a process than a place; a series of tests and interviews with job candidates that can stretch over a number of days. An attempt to improve upon the more normal method of job selection based on a single sheet of typescript (the candidate's curriculum vitae) and a short INTERVIEW.

ASSETS

Anything that a COMPANY (or an individual) owns that can be given a monetary VALUE. That includes intangible things like GOODWILL.

A company's assets are listed on the left-hand side of its BALANCE SHEET, except in the UK where the LIABILITIES (like the traffic) tend to go on the left. They are further divided into fixed assets (which are not easy to move) and current assets (which are).

Assets are notorious for being stripped. "Asset stripping" is a financially sophisticated sleight-of-hand which relies on the fact that the value of the assets on a company's balance sheet (net of its liabilities) is sometimes higher than the value of its shares on the STOCKMARKET. Under those circumstances a so-called "asset stripper" can make a successful bid for the company's shares, sell off all its assets, and be left with a tidy PROFIT. Asset strippers are not considered to be of great value to industrial society.

> *No one has a greater asset for*
> *his business than a man's pride*
> *in his work.*
> Mary Parker Follett

ASSOCIATED COMPANY

Company A is an associated COMPANY of Company B if more than 20%, but less than 50%, of its equity is owned by Company B. This makes the relationship between the two companies less than that between a holding company and its SUBSIDIARY. It is a more significant relationship than that between an ordinary investor and the company in which he or she holds shares.

Companies do not need to consolidate associated companies in their ACCOUNTS unless they CONTROL the composition of the BOARD of directors of the associated company, in which case it is deemed to be a subsidiary.

AUDIT/AUDITOR

Almost everywhere a COMPANY's ACCOUNTS are required to be inspected and checked by an outside independent firm of recognised accountants, or by a special government body set up for the purpose. This inspection is called an audit, and the inspectors are called auditors.

Auditing is an old business; the word is derived from the Latin for hearing. In olden days it referred to the "hearing" that the owner of land gave to the manager in which the manager would account for his stewardship. Nowadays auditors are appointed by shareholders and report to them. Their report may be either "clean" or "qualified". It will be qualified if the auditors have been unable to satisfy themselves on any issue that they are legally obliged to check. Companies go to great lengths to avoid the stigma of a qualified audit.

An auditor's main concern is to see whether the accounts represent a "true and fair view" of the company's affairs. "True and fair" is the central principle of accounting, and there is a general assumption that there is only one true and fair view of things. But accountants can (and do) easily disagree about what is true and about what is fair, so any audit that is deemed clean by one reputable accountant could truly and fairly be qualified by another.

In recent years the word has taken on a wider meaning. Companies have "internal audits", that is, inspections of the accounts carried out by a committee or individual from inside the business. And they have "environmental audits" to check that the company is complying with environmental legislation and doing what it can to avoid pollution. Next will come "human-resource audits".

AUFSICHTSRAT

The supervisory BOARD, mandatory for the many German companies that have to have two boards: a supervisory board and a MANAGEMENT board (*VORSTAND*). Members of the *Aufsichtsrat* are elected by shareholders; and one of their main responsibilities is the election of members of the *Vorstand*.

AUTOMATION

The process of replacing human LABOUR with machines. Early automation aroused strong reactions. The Luddites, who were a group of nineteenth-century workers, wilfully destroyed FACTORY machines in the north of England on the grounds that they took away their livelihood. Their name has gone into the dictionary.

Modern automation has focused on ROBOTICS, the use of COMPUTER-driven robots to perform industrial tasks with an absolute minimum of human intervention. Robotics has been widely introduced into the car industry, and has on occasions aroused reactions only slightly less vehement than the Luddites.

INFORMATION TECHNOLOGY, the combination of telecommunications and computers, is seen by some as the first form of automation that does not threaten human labour. The argument is that the wider dissemination of information throughout corporations (which is the consequence of information technology) requires more (and better) human intervention in order to interpret and make use of it for the benefit of the corporation.

It was naive of nineteenth-century optimists to expect paradise from technology, and it is equally naive of twentieth-century pessimists to make technology the scapegoat for such old shortcomings as man's blindness, cruelty, immaturity, greed and sinful pride.
Peter Drucker

BACK-TO-BACK

A financial arrangement in which a COMPANY, A, lends a sum of money to another company B (or to a SUBSIDIARY of B) at the same time as B lends an equal amount to A.

Put like that it all sounds a bit pointless, but back-to-back loans can be mutually advantageous to both A and B if, for example, they are based in different countries. Suppose A is French and B is German. If A lends French francs to B's French operation (which it needs for working CAPITAL) while B lends Deutschemarks to A (for buying German exports), then both companies have got hold of necessary foreign exchange without having to buy it expensively from banks.

BACK-UP

The essential business of arranging for a COMPUTER system to make copies of data that are being stored in it. Despite the marvels of modern silicon technology it is still as easy (if not easier) to lose a computer file as it is to lose a paper one. More often the loss is the result of human error, but there are still occasions when computer files disappear spontaneously into thin air for what can only be termed "technological reasons".

BALANCE SHEET

The statement of a COMPANY's ASSETS and LIABILITIES. The balance sheet and the PROFIT AND LOSS ACCOUNT are the backbone of a company's annual report: the yearly account of themselves made by the managers of a company to its owners.

The balance sheet is a sort of snapshot of the worth of a company at close of play on one particular day. It is a blurred snapshot, however, for several reasons.

Some assets cannot be valued by accountants, so they do not appear on the balance sheet. Others that do can be tarted up for the day (see WINDOW-DRESSING) and can look very different the morning after.

EUROPEAN COMMUNITY legislation has introduced a standard format for balance sheets across

Europe, but it will be some time before different countries' ACCOUNTS are sufficiently similar for valid cross-country comparisons to be widely made. For the moment do not assume that an Italian's assets are equal to anybody else's.

BANKER'S DRAFT

A useful way of financing trade between two parties who do not know each other, a banker's draft is a sort of cheque written by a bank on itself. A DEBTOR buys one from a bank and gives it to their CREDITOR when the creditor will not accept the debtor's own cheque. Assuming that the bank itself is not about to go bust, a banker's draft is as good as cash.

The banker's draft provides a vivid example of the way in which banks make money out of people's distrust of each other. When companies have more trust in, say, IBM than they have in their bank, then they begin to cut their bank out of their business, a process that is called disintermediation.

If you owe your bank £100, you have a problem. But if you owe it £1m then it has.
John Maynard Keynes

BANKRUPTCY

The condition of being bankrupt. A DEBTOR becomes bankrupt when the courts agree to a request from him or her (or from an unpaid CREDITOR) to be declared insolvent; that is, unable to pay debts when they become due. The courts then appoint an official to assess the bankrupt person's ASSETS and LIABILITIES, and to apportion them (apart from clothing and the tools of their trade) to his or her creditors.

When this has been completed to the court's satisfaction the bankrupt will be discharged. Until that time such people are known as "undischarged bankrupts". There are tight restrictions on what undischarged bankrupts may do.

BAR CHART

A simple graphical way of representing a series of data which measure the same thing under different circumstances. For example, the maximum temperature in a number of different countries; or the average COST of living in different large cities. The bar chart and the PIE CHART are the most commonly used charts in business.

BAR CODING

The series of vertical lines of differing thickness that appear on the packaging of most products today. Bar coding enables electronic scanners at the POINT OF SALE to read several details about the product (including its price) without the cashier having to key anything time-consumingly into a machine. Bar coding is also helpful in stock CONTROL.

BARTER

The direct exchange of goods for other goods, a form of trading that is at least as old as money itself. Barter is unpopular with banks since it reduces the need for their services, but it is often popular with businesses. They can use it to avoid tax if the goods are not converted into their monetary VALUE (and hence do not pass through the PROFIT AND LOSS ACCOUNT). Tax authorities, naturally, demand that all barter deals be converted for accounting purposes. (See also COUNTERTRADE.)

BATCH

A bunch of things that have something in common. The word is used commercially in such phrases as the following.

• **Batch processing.** This is the gathering of COMPUTER data in batches before they are processed; an alternative to processing each bit of data singly (and inefficiently) as and when it is ready.
• **Batch production.** A method of manufacturing things in batches that falls somewhere between MASS PRODUCTION and handicraft.

BEARER BOND

A BOND that belongs to whoever "bears" it, that is whoever has the bond document in their hand; in contrast to normal bonds whose rightful owner is registered with the issuer of the bond. A bearer bond usually comes with a book of coupons attached. The coupons are handed in on their due date in order to claim the interest payments on the bond.

Bonds issued in the EUROMARKET are always issued in bearer form. They have the great MARKETING advantage of being virtually untraceable by tax inspectors.

BELOW-THE-LINE

An accounting expression that refers to items in the PROFIT AND LOSS ACCOUNT that appear below the net PROFIT figure. The opposite of ABOVE-THE-LINE.

BILL OF EXCHANGE

Confirmation of a debt between two companies that is due to be paid at a future date, usually in 30, 60 or 90 days. The maturity varies according to common commercial practice in different countries. In Belgium, for example, the maturity is more usually 30 days, whereas in the UK it is more commonly 90 days.

Bills of exchange have been popular since the fifteenth century. They were introduced by Italian traders and copied by their Flemish counterparts. They have developed into negotiable instruments that can be "accepted" (see ACCEPTANCE CREDIT) by a bank and then turned into ready cash. This separation of the money underlying a commercial transaction from the transaction itself is seen as a major step in the development of capitalism.

BILL OF LADING

The document given by a shipping or trucking COMPANY to the person whose goods it is transporting. The bill of lading acknowledges the amount of freight received, the condition it is in, and the terms under which it is being transported.

If the shipping company receives the freight in good condition then it gives a clean bill (as in "a clean bill of health"). If, however, it inserts a clause saying that the freight was not received as it should be, then the bill is known as a dirty bill of lading.

For the person whose goods are being shipped, the bill of lading is documentary proof of ownership. As such it can be used as security, for example, to DISCOUNT a bill of exchange received from the purchaser of the goods.

There are many different types of bill, most of them relating to the form of transport of the goods; for example, inland waterways bill, railway bill, liner bill, and so on.

BINARY SYSTEM

For no more special reason than the fact that we have ten fingers, our mathematics is based on the decimal system, that is on the number ten. Hence the number 2,451 is actually $2 \times 10^3 + 4 \times 10^2 + 5 \times 10^1 + 1 \times 10^0$.

We could base our mathematics on any number; the number two, for instance. In such a system, instead of needing ten digits (0-9) we need only two (1 and 0). 10,010 then becomes equal to $1 \times 2^4 + 0 \times 2^3 + 0.2^2 + 1 \times 2^1 + 0 \times 2^0$. In the decimal system that is 16 + 2, or 18.

A system based on two digits is called a binary system. It becomes particularly useful in electronics and COMPUTERS where switches are either on or off, and currents either flow or they do not flow. An "off" switch can represent 0 and an "on" switch 1. Rows and rows of switches can then be used to do all sorts of computations. (Note that mathematical operations are carried out in the binary system in the same way as in the decimal system. So 10,010 + 11,101 = 101,111; or 18 + 29 = 47.)

BIOTECHNOLOGY

A technology based on the use of living organisms to produce chemical changes and new materials. Biotechnology was believed (at the beginning of the 1980s) to hold great promise for the production of new products, and of new ways to make old products (like insulin and antibiotics).

One branch, called genetic engineering, produced changes by reorganising the genetic structure of different life forms. Not surprisingly it raised fears that communities might be in danger from the accidental escape of mutant life forms. So far such fears have been unfounded, except in the imaginations of Hollywood scriptwriters.

Despite attracting much venture CAPITAL, the biotechnology industry has yet to fulfil its promise.

BLACK ECONOMY

That considerable portion of a nation's income that does not show up in official statistics because it is not recorded in individual or corporate tax returns.

The size of the black economy varies. In the USA it is reckoned to be less than 5% of GDP; in Italy some estimates put it as high as 25%. In very low-income developing countries it may be even higher; who knows what economic activity takes place unrecorded in, say, Myanmar.

Since a major factor behind the black economy in developed countries is tax evasion, it should decrease in size with decreases in tax rates. In the UK in the 1980s, however, when personal tax rates fell steeply under the Thatcher government, the black economy did not appear to shrink.

BLUE-COLLAR WORKER

A reference to the blue clothes that it was once customary for workers to wear on the factory floor. Contrasted with WHITE-COLLAR WORKER, and yet another example of the colourful use of language in business – along with blue chip, gilt-edged, red tape, in the red, BROWN GOODS, WHITE GOODS, green audit, blackleg and BLACK ECONOMY.

BOARD

The committee of directors officially appointed by

the shareholders of a COMPANY to look after their interests. Many boards are called upon to do little more than meet once a month in the boardroom – a hallowed place that at other times remains uselessly empty – and then to enjoy a good lunch.

Keeping the board minutes (the record of the meeting) is one of the most important parts of the ritual of these monthly gatherings.

Many boards are self-perpetuating oligarchies, selecting new directors from among their own close acquaintances.

Shareholders have the right to reject the board's recommendations, but they rarely exercise that right. By and large, shareholders get the boards that they deserve.

Countries like Germany and Sweden have two-tier boards: a management board made up of executive directors who "direct" the company's day-to-day business; and a supervisory board, made up of non-executives who "supervise" the management board.

The most striking difference between this board structure and the Anglo-Saxon structure is not so much its duality as the fact that on management boards sit company workers, or their representatives.

What goes on in the boardroom is a travesty. The chairman doesn't want someone under him who is a threat, so he picks someone a little less capable. It's like an anti-Darwinian theory – the survival of the unfittest – and it's getting worse.
Carl Icahn, corporate raider, 1985

BOND

In its widest sense, any document which acknowledges the existence of a debt. In financial markets a bond is a fixed-interest security maturing in a stated time and issued by a government or corporation. Many such bonds are traded on the STOCKMARKET. They can change hands many times before they mature and are "redeemed" at their "face VALUE".

Bonds come in many shapes and sizes.

- **BEARER BOND**.
- **Convertible bond.** A bond which may be exchanged for shares (or some other sort of security) after a certain amount of time and at the bondholder's discretion.
- **Indexed bond.** A bond whose interest payments and CAPITAL value are adjusted according to the rate of inflation.
- **Irredeemable bond.** Sometimes known as an annuity bond or perpetual bond; a bond that has no maturity date and on which interest is payable ad infinitum; it comes close to being the same as EQUITY.
- **Junk bond.** A bond that is a load of rubbish, or (more technically) a bond issued by a corporation that has less than a given CREDIT RATING from the major US credit-rating agencies (Moody's and Standard & Poor's).
- **Performance bond.** A pledge given by contractors that they will pay a certain sum of money should they fail to perform according to their CONTRACT.
- **Redeemable bond.** A bond that may be repaid by the issuer when he or she wishes, on giving a certain amount of notice.
- **Savings bond.** A savings instrument issued by governments to encourage small savers. It usually comes with tax advantages attached.

BONDED WAREHOUSE

A guarded warehouse in which importers can store goods duty-free. The importers withdraw their goods (and pay duty on them) as and when they need them.

Bonded warehouses are often run by governments. When owned by a private firm, that firm gives the government a "bond" (or pledge) that it will faithfully carry out its duty (of ensuring that duty is paid on the goods).

BONUS

An extra payment made to employees or agents over and above what they can contractually expect. In some countries bonus payments to employees are regular and substantial; in Germany, for instance, almost all employees get a bonus at Christmas and in the summer. Each bonus can amount to a full month's salary, giving many Germans 14 months' pay per annum. In other countries bonuses are rare.

A "bonus issue" is an issue of shares made to existing shareholders free of charge. However, these may not be as much of a bonus as they sound. When a COMPANY issues new shares for free, the VALUE of its existing shares falls. A bonus issue merely divides a cake of a given size into more pieces.

BOOK-KEEPING

The art of keeping a COMPANY's books, that is, recording the day-to-day transactions of the company in financial terms. These books form the basis of the company's annual accounts. (See also DOUBLE-ENTRY.)

BOYCOTT

An organised attempt not to trade with a particular person, COMPANY or country. Boycotts are notoriously difficult to enforce. TRADE UNIONS and pressure groups have occasionally tried to boycott companies whose policies they disapprove of, but such companies nearly always find somebody who is willing to do business with them, at a price.

Country boycotts are similarly difficult to enforce. The boycott of Rhodesia – before it became Zimbabwe – is a classic case. Rhodesia was able to get almost all it needed through neighbouring South Africa.

BRANDING

The attribution to a product of a name or TRADE-MARK which, in the extreme, becomes almost synonymous with the product, as Coke is to cola.

Companies with a strong brand have a valuable asset. An IBM COMPUTER can be sold for more than an identical computer without the famous three-letter acronym. Some companies try to put a VALUE in their BALANCE SHEET on the premium that they are able to charge because of their brand names.

Research into Europe's most powerful brands shows that many of them are cars: Mercedes-Benz, Rolls-Royce and Ferrari, for example. Non-car names that appear high on the list include Adidas and Nescafé.

The value of brand names in CONSUMER goods is being eroded by retailers' "own label" products. Sainsbury's beans now compete with Heinz's, for example, because the Sainsbury name is as highly thought of as Heinz, and its prices are lower.

BROKER
An intermediary who is employed by a COMPANY or person to trade on their behalf, usually in return for a fee or a percentage commission.

Brokers do not own the goods that they buy and sell, unlike "dealers" who actually buy goods before selling them on to somebody else.

Brokers come in at least 57 varieties.

• **Commodity brokers.** Act as agents for buyers and sellers in different commodity markets; either the metal markets, or the markets for "soft commodities" like coffee, cotton and wheat.
• **Insurance brokers.** Advise clients on the best companies for particular insurance contracts. Although they are not employed by insurance companies, the broker's income usually comes as commissions from the insurer.
• **Pawnbrokers.** People who lend money on the security of personal property that is deposited with them. The property can be retrieved once the loan and interest have been repaid in full within an agreed time limit.
• **Shipbrokers.** Go-betweens for shipowners and for those who want cargo (or passengers) shipped.
• **Stockbrokers.** Buy stocks and shares on

behalf of clients. On many stock exchanges stockbrokers used to be strictly separated from dealers in stocks and shares. That distinction has been eliminated recently in many markets.

He's called a broker because after dealing with him you are.
Aphorism

BROWN GOODS

An expression beloved by MARKETING people and ADVERTISING agencies. It refers to electrical goods that were traditionally sold to consumers in brown casings, such as radios, televisions, record players, and so on. Now, of course, they are mostly sold in black casings, but they are still brown goods. (See also WHITE GOODS.)

BUDGETING

The process of producing budgets – forecasts of likely future income and expenditure – as a basis for planning how to allocate COMPANY resources, like cash and employees. Budgets are usually drawn up for a full year. Their preparation can lead to the almost total exclusion of any other activity.

Computers are changing the budgeting process. They are turning what used to be a very long drawn-out and rigid affair into something fast and flexible. That means more choices, but it does not necessarily mean better choices.

A budget is a numerical check of your worst suspicions.
Anon

BUFFER STOCK

In general, a stock of materials that is held in reserve at every stage of a production process; spares kept just in case there are delays in the supply of materials. It is expensive to sit on a permanent buffer stock just in case of a rainy day, so modern stock-CONTROL methods aim to cut buffer stocks down to a minimum. Such methods aim to supplant "just-in-case" with "JUST-IN-TIME".

More specifically, buffer stocks are stocks held in reserve by the managers of international commodity agreements. Countries which depend heavily on a single commodity for their export earnings (such as Zambia with its copper) get together and agree to maintain stocks of the commodity in order to stabilise its price.

The exporters argue that this is in the best interests of their customers. But commodity buffer stocks have almost invariably got into difficulties. In 1986 the International Tin Agreement (ITA) fell apart when the manager of the buffer stock bought so much tin that he ran out of money. The major tin-producing countries (like Malaysia) then refused to give him any more.

BUSINESS CYCLE

Businesses and national economies do not grow steadily in a straight line for ever (although observers of the 1980s might be forgiven for having believed briefly that they do). Like the rest of us, business and trade go in cycles. They rise to a peak of activity before falling back into a recessionary sleep. They then wake up to begin the cycle all over again.

This is a finding based on past experience, but there is nothing to guarantee that it will continue to happen. Since the second world war the cycles' periodicity in the western world has been around five years. But in the 1980s almost ten years passed between the trough of 1981 and the next major trough of 1990–91.

People have attempted to link the business cycle to things like the weather, or the effect of sunspots on harvests. A Russian economist, Nikolai Kondratieff, identified much longer cycles of some 50–60 years on which shorter cycles were superimposed. Kondratieff published his findings in the 1920s, before the Great Depression of the early 1930s, almost exactly 60 years ago.

B

*The majority of businessmen are incapable of
original thought because they are unable to
escape from the tyranny of reason.*
David Ogilvy

BUSINESS SYSTEM

A way of looking at a business as a sequence of
activities, each of which can be costed and analysed vis-à-vis the same activity in the business's
rivals. The system was developed and widely
used by McKinsey's, a firm of MANAGEMENT consultants, and provided the basis for Professor
Michael Porter's theory about the VALUE CHAIN.

BY-PRODUCT

Something sellable that is produced as an incidental side-effect of the manufacture of a main
product; sawdust by the carpenter, for example.
In one sense the whole of the natural gas industry
is only a by-product of the oil business.

By-products used to be considered rather inferior things; in the verbal wars between butter and
margarine, butter-lovers would maintain that margarine was a mere by-product from the manufacture of soap powder. (Unilever makes both.)
By-products have recently been changing their
image. Industry is increasingly looking to them to
help recycle waste produced by its main manufacturing processes.

BYTE

A unit for measuring the storage capacity of a
COMPUTER. One byte equals eight bits, and a bit is
a single binary digit (see BINARY SYSTEM). Even
portable computers nowadays have a storage
capacity of several million bytes.

C

CAPACITY

The amount that a FACTORY or plant can produce in a given time. Most factories are working "below full capacity", if only because there are always some workers and machines in need of repair. When order-books are empty then the "surplus capacity" of the factory rises. The ratio of surplus capacity to full capacity is a closely watched figure.

CAPITAL

> *Capital is dead labour that, vampire-like, lives only by sucking living labour, and lives the more, the more labour it sucks.*
> Karl Marx, *Das Kapital*

> *Capital is that part of the wealth of a country which is employed in production and consists of food, clothing, tools, raw materials, etc, necessary to give effect to labour.*
> David Ricardo

As these quotations from two great economists demonstrate, capital looks different from different angles. From one angle it is one of the three factors of production (along with LABOUR and land). On the other hand managers talk of human capital, the people who work in their business, and investors talk of share capital, the amount of money put into a COMPANY to buy its shares.

Some other uses of a word which occurs widely in many languages are as follows.

● **Authorised capital.** The maximum amount of share capital that a company is authorised to raise by its memorandum and articles of association.
● **Called-up capital.** The amount of capital that shareholders have been asked to pay. This can be less than the issued capital (see below) because some share issues will only require investors to pay in instalments over a period of time.

- **Flight capital.** Money which leaves a country because of political or economic difficulties in order to find a safe haven elsewhere. The irony of flight capital is that it tends to leave the places that need it most (unsettled developing countries) and go to the places that need it least (Switzerland or the Cayman Islands).
- **Issued capital.** The amount of capital actually issued to investors in the form of shares. This can never be greater than the authorised capital.
- **Paid-up capital.** The amount of capital actually paid for by investors. This is less than the issued capital by the amount that shareholders have been asked for, but have not yet paid.
- **Seed capital.** See SEED MONEY.
- **Start-up capital.** The money needed to get a project off the ground. It may be just enough to do a bit of MARKET RESEARCH to show that the business has potential. That then convinces banks or other investors to put up the rest of the money that the business needs.
- **Venture capital.** This used to be known as risk capital, as if there were some sort of capital that did not have any risk. There is not (not even savings in a bank), but venture capital does have more risk than most. It is money that goes into new ventures, often HIGH-TECH ones, whose future is very uncertain. For this high risk, investors in venture capital expect high returns.
- **WORKING CAPITAL.**

If only Groucho had written Das Kapital.
Graffiti

CAPITAL INTENSIVE
The description of industries which need a lot of CAPITAL to start them up and to keep them going. Such industries include those requiring sophisticated digging in the ground (such as the oil industry) or considerable infrastructure (such as railways). The high capital requirement acts as a

---

barrier to entry into the industry; not everyone can open an oil refinery tomorrow.

Some businesses require very little capital (for example, service industries like ADVERTISING and accounting). They are referred to as LABOUR-intensive, and are being continually revived by people breaking away from old firms to start new ones. Who last started a steel business?

CAPITAL MARKETS

These are markets for the long-term funds needed for CAPITAL investment, either to expand existing business projects or to start new ones. Capital markets can be divided into two.

● **Primary markets.** In which new money is actually raised from investors in the form of shares, bonds or long-term bank loans. Companies in different countries raise long-term capital from these sources in varying proportions. German and Japanese companies are more dependent on bank loans; UK and US companies more on shares.
● **Secondary markets.** In which investors trade their shares or bonds and sell them to somebody else. Only bank loans cannot in general be traded, but even then there are exceptions. In the 1980s there was a thriving secondary market in long-term bank loans to developing countries.

This is a very clever system. It gives those raising the capital the security of knowing that they have funds for a long period. Yet it allows investors to get out of their investment immediately if they so wish, by selling on the secondary market. Nevertheless there is a continuing conflict between the "short-termism" that this encourages among investors, and the "long-termism" that is the real need of industry.

Capitalism without bankruptcy is like Christianity without hell.
Frank Borman, CEO of Eastern Airlines

CARTEL

The formal organisation of a group of manufacturers with the express purpose of reducing COMPETITION between them by, for example, fixing prices. The most famous cartel is the ORGANISATION OF PETROLEUM EXPORTING COUNTRIES (OPEC). Cartels attempt to give themselves the economic benefits of a MONOPOLY, but when push comes to shove they are only as strong as their weakest member.

Cartels are like babies; we tend to be against them until we have one of our own.

Anon

CASH BOOK

The book of ACCOUNTS that records a COMPANY's cash transactions, including those in and out of its bank accounts.

CASH FLOW

A statement of the amount of cash flowing into a COMPANY during a specified period. This can be calculated from the accountants' concept of net PROFIT. Subtract the amount paid in dividends from the net profit, and then add back non-cash expenses that have been subtracted, such as DEPRECIATION. Finally, subtract non-cash revenues like deferred income. And there you have it.

Cash flow is an important indicator of a company's ability to pay future dividends and of its ability to finance future investment from its own resources. It is a cheaper source of funds than expensive bank loans or rights issues.

Some companies (like General Electric and the big Japanese car and electronics firms) have enormous cash flows that they are unable to invest. That leaves them looking rather like banks, holding huge deposits of other people's (that is, their shareholders') money. Strange that they never think of giving it back to the shareholders, for them to invest.

Ways to improve cash flow include the following.

❏ Make special bank arrangements to speed up transfers of funds between accounts.
❏ Offer cash discounts for early payment.
❏ Send invoices out more quickly.
❏ Telephone reminders.
❏ Demand cash on delivery.
❏ Minimise cash tied up elsewhere (in loans to staff, for instance).

CASH ON DELIVERY

Cash on delivery (COD) indicates that a transaction requires cash (or an equivalent) to be paid for goods at the place and time that they are delivered to the purchaser. The US term is collect on delivery.

CATCH 22

The title of a novel by Joseph Heller that has become a catch-phrase for situations that can also be described as "Heads I win, tails you lose". Commonly found where there are restrictive employment practices; for example, people cannot work as journalists until they are members of the journalists' union, but to join the union they have to have worked as journalists.

CENTRALISATION

The process of concentrating CONTROL of an organisation at its centre. The opposite of delegation. Centralisation is currently unfashionable as a MANAGEMENT style, but it is frequently found in companies that are driven largely by the efforts of one person.

It may be a mistake to consider centralisation and decentralisation as mutually exclusive. Hanson, a very successful conglomerate, combines the two. Tight centralised control of BUDGETING leads to decentralised control of the methods of achieving the budget's targets.

C

Responsibility is the great developer of men.
Mary Parker Follett

CERTIFICATE OF ORIGIN

A formal document stating the country of origin of exported goods, signed either by the exporter or by an official body (like a chamber of commerce).

Certificates of origin are increasingly important in the EUROPEAN COMMUNITY where goods imported into one member state may be freely exported to another. There they will be treated differently depending on whether they originated in the other member state, or were just passing through on their way from a non-member state.

CHAIRMAN

The person in charge of the meetings of a company's BOARD. The chairman also has the casting vote should the directors of the board be evenly split on a decision.

Many company chairmen are also the company's chief executive, a combination of duties that is increasingly being questioned. The chairman of the board is theoretically the leading representative of the company's shareholders; the chief executive is the leading representative of the managers and other employees. It is a lot to expect one person to play both roles in the best interests of both groups.

CHAPTER 11

Part of the USA's 1978 Bankruptcy Act, providing a novel approach to troubled companies. Before Chapter 11 was written a troubled company's creditors either got everything back because the company got itself out of trouble; or they got virtually nothing because the company collapsed. It was an all-or-nothing affair, with no options in between.

Chapter 11 provided options by allowing the DEBTOR company and its creditors to work together to find a solution. A solution could involve the creditors in agreeing to take, say, 40% of what they were owed, and agreeing to write off the rest.

The idea behind Chapter 11 was followed in the UK (where it is called ADMINISTRATION) and elsewhere. In the USA, however, the process was criticised following cases like that of Manville Corporation, an asbestos company that sought the protection of Chapter 11 because it said that its liability for asbestos-induced diseases among its employees could force it into LIQUIDATION.

Is Chapter 11 what comes after following the ten commandments?

CHARGE
Not just what an aggressive COMPANY does when entering a new MARKET; nor just the price of a service (note that lawyers and accountants have charges; chemists and newsagents have prices). A charge (or lien) is also a form of security taken by a lender over property that has been purchased by the borrower (often a home purchased with a mortgage). Such a charge has to be registered with an official body. If the borrower fails to meet the conditions of the loan agreement, the lender can take possession of the property over which it has the charge. (See also FLOATING CHARGE.)

CHECKLIST
The all too frequently inane listing of the essential elements of an issue. For example, in successful takeovers somebody has suggested that it is essential to:

❏ have a strategic purpose;
❏ know the business;
❏ investigate thoroughly;
❏ make realistic assumptions;
❏ not pay too much;
❏ not borrow too much;
❏ integrate carefully and quickly.

C

Checklists like this are an attempt to save managers from "wasting" time on thinking; but those for whom thinking is a waste of time should not be managers.

CIF
See COST, INSURANCE, FREIGHT.

CLOSED SHOP
The situation where LABOUR unions have compelled managers to agree that nobody who is not a member of their union may be employed in a particular business or FACTORY. Closed shops are not just operated by traditionally bolshy groups like journalists and builders. Though more discreet, the professional associations of accountants, lawyers and doctors frequently have much the same effect as the closed shop of the BLUE-COLLAR WORKER.

COD
See CASH ON DELIVERY.

COLLATERAL
Something that a borrower provides (over and above a trustworthy smile) as security for a loan. If the lender does not get the loan back it can take the collateral instead. Collateral is commonly held in the form of a CHARGE over property, but it can be in the form of bearer bonds, or other sorts of title to property, held by the lender until it is repaid in full.

COLLECTIVE BARGAINING
The process of negotiating wage and salary increases collectively rather than individually. This involves (sometimes lengthy) negotiations between TRADE UNIONS and employers. Most PUBLIC-SECTOR employees' pay is determined by collective bargaining. In the PRIVATE SECTOR, on the other hand, most managers' salaries are determined by individual negotiation.

In Germany the annual collective bargaining process is a sophisticated ritual which sometimes sets new benchmarks for employment practice. In 1990 industry agreed to union demands for the standard working week to be cut from 37 hours to 35 hours by 1995.

COMMERCIAL PAPER

A short-term debt instrument popular in the USA. Commercial paper has a maturity of 2–270 days, although the most popular maturities lie within 30–90 days. Commercial paper does not usually pay interest. Rather, it is sold at a DISCOUNT, with the full amount repayable on maturity.

Commercial paper is issued by big well-known industrial and financial corporations and, by and large, is also bought by big well-known industrial and financial corporations. It is not designed for small private investors, since it is usually issued in minimum dollops of $100,000.

A committee is an animal with four back legs.
John Le Carré

COMPANY

A legal entity formed by a group of individuals for the purpose of doing business. The company is recognised in law as a separate entity having rights and duties distinct from those of the individuals who form it. They can all die, yet the company continues to exist.

The most significant right for most companies is that of LIMITED LIABILITY. The duties that go with that right are numerous and laid down in company law. They include restrictions on what directors can do, and requirements to register information so that it is accessible to the general public.

Within that framework there are many different types of company.

● **AFFILIATE.**
● **ASSOCIATED COMPANY.**
● **Chartered company.** In the UK a company

formed by royal charter rather than by registration under the Companies Acts.

- **Holding company.** A company, sometimes called a parent company, formed for the purpose of owning one or more other companies. All the companies together constitute a group.
- **Joint-stock company.** A company whose CAPITAL is divided into small units of stock (that is, shares) that can be bought and sold.
- **Private company.** A company that is not allowed to sell its shares to the general public nor to raise capital from the general public.
- **PUBLIC COMPANY.**
- **QUOTED COMPANY.**
- **Shell company.** What is left after a company has had all its assets "stripped" (see ASSETS).
- **SUBSIDIARY.**
- **Unlimited company.** The very rare case where the owners of a company have unlimited liability. In such cases it is usually more appropriate to set up a PARTNERSHIP than a company.

The great modern corporations are so similar to independent or semi-independent states of the past that they can only be fully understood in terms of political and constitutional history, and management can only be properly studied as a branch of government.

Anthony Jay

COMPATIBLE

What bits and pieces of computers are when they can be linked up and worked together; for instance, a printer is IBM compatible when it can print material from an IBM PC.

COMPETITION

The eternal contest between business firms to see which can perform the best either in terms of MARKET share, PROFIT, or some other recognised yardstick. The nature of this struggle is coloured by national heritage: for the British it is like crick-

C

et or hunting (playing the game is at least as important as winning); for the Americans it is a perpetual replay of a John Wayne movie.

Competition is rarely pure and unqualified.

● **Cut-throat competition.** A blood-curdling concept that goes back to the military origins of MANAGEMENT. Usually refers to situations where supply exceeds demand; and suppliers cut prices to maintain their share of a market, well aware that some of their competitors must collapse.

● **Healthy competition.** Competition between firms that are not believed to be indulging in unfair practices.

● **Monopolistic competition.** Sounds like a contradiction in terms, for is MONOPOLY not the absence of competition? But this is an economists' expression, and for them it means something between a total monopoly and perfect competition (see below); that is, virtually all of business life.

● **Perfect competition.** The theoretical economists' Valhalla where a large number of buyers and sellers of a homogeneous product ensure that no one of them can affect its price. Firms maximise their profits by producing just enough goods to make their marginal COST equal to their marginal revenue.

● **Unfair competition.** Where manufacturers make dishonest claims about a product, for example. Much competition that is described as unfair is not. To the western world the Japanese are terribly unfair. For example, they "dump" products on new markets at prices that are below cost. But is that unfair, or is it a legitimate "special introductory offer", or "loss leader"? Not even the Japanese can sell below cost for long.

Competition brings out the best in products and the worst in people.
David Sarnoff, former president of RCA

COMPUTER
The computer has been to the twentieth century

what the steam engine was to the nineteenth. Yet nobody has won a Nobel prize for its invention. It has crept, not leapt into our lives.

The computer is a machine that harnesses the physics of electronics, the chemistry of silicon, and the mathematics of the BINARY SYSTEM. It uses them to store information, to process it, and then to perform an infinitely large number of tasks with a speed and efficiency which, without the benefit of hindsight, we might have assumed would by now have made us all redundant.

In fact the opposite has occurred. In industries like banking and accounting, where the computer has obvious potential to reduce employment, the workforce has increased dramatically since its invention. In industry and commerce, computers are used in all sorts of ways: as calculators in the accounts department; as robots in the production department; and as typewriters in head office.

There are all sorts of them.

- **LAPTOP computers.**
- **Mainframe computers.** The old-fashioned giants that used to sit in the COMPANY's basement, were operated by boffins, and were sometimes rented out at weekends.
- **Minicomputers.** Smaller than a mainframe but with a central processor powerful enough to service a NETWORK.
- **Personal computers.** Known as PCs, these are the sort of computers that sit comfortably on one person's desk, and are sometimes light enough to be carried around.
- **Supercomputers.** Extra powerful machines that use the latest computer technology to perform amazingly complex operations amazingly fast.

One computer manufacturer was so successful he had to move to smaller premises.
Anon

CONCENTRATION

There is a tendency for industrial sectors in developed economies to become increasingly dominated by a few large firms. Activity becomes "concentrated" in their hands. In the oil industry the concentration in the hands of the "Seven Sisters" is well-known. In Europe it is evident in banking, where the business is heavily concentrated in the hands of three or four almost indistinguishable institutions in France, Germany and the UK.

No COMPANY ever had the ambition to become smaller; so the tendency to concentration is in-built. It is held in check to some extent by laws which prevent takeovers from giving one firm a "dominant share" of any particular MARKET.

Karl Marx thought that concentration would be the ruin of capitalism, creating a small elite and a vast exploited mass which would eventually rise up in revolt. In the event he got the right cause but the wrong effect. The concentration of power and resources in the hands of East European elites was the ruin of communism.

CONCESSION

A special right given to somebody, usually for a price, not always paid in cash. For example:

- the exclusive right to sell the products of a manufacturer within a certain area;
- the right to dig for minerals on a particular plot of land;
- a tax allowance given to encourage things like exports and investment in underdeveloped regions.

CONGLOMERATE

A COMPANY that is in a large number of different businesses, not all of which seem to fit logically with each other. Such companies present a challenge to journalists' descriptive powers. "The fags-to-bags group" is one attempt for B.A.T, which makes cigarettes and paper (and lots of other things besides). (See DIVERSIFICATION.)

C

If you want to control it, own it.
Gospel of the conglomerates of the 1960s

CONSIGNMENT
A bunch of goods consigned (sent) from one place to another. Goods sent "on consignment" to an AGENT by a manufacturer are goods that have been sent on a sale-or-return basis. Agents do not pay for them until they sell them, and any that they do not sell are returned to sender.

CONSOLIDATION
A method of treating a group – that is, a parent COMPANY and its subsidiaries – as a single unit for accounting purposes. In most developed countries consolidation is now a legal requirement for large companies.

Consolidation developed in the English-speaking business world to meet the demands of investors for a complete picture of the company that they owned. In extremis a parent company might exist only to hold the shares of its subsidiaries. Without consolidation its ACCOUNTS would be just a list of its shareholdings. Through consolidation shareholders would get an idea of the businesses the subsidiaries were actually in.

It is less popular in continental Europe where legal considerations are more influential than investors' fancy. A group does not actually exist as a legal entity; you cannot sue it. And the tax inspector does not assess it for tax; the taxable entity is each individual corporation. So why draw up accounts for it?

Consolidation is a rather complicated process that involves adding together ASSETS and LIABILITIES, and revenues and expenses, of the parent and its subsidiaries. Bits here and there are then subtracted to avoid double-counting transactions between companies within the group. The ways in which companies consolidate subsidiaries in different countries are very inconsistent, but then they are often inconsistent within the same country.

CONSORTIUM

The combination of a number of large companies for the purposes of one specific project. This is commonly done for very large building projects – like dams and bridges – which are too large for one company to undertake alone. Consortia are useful too when a number of specialist skills are needed for a job that cannot be found within a single firm.

This was the logic behind consortium banks, popular in the 1970s and early 1980s. They brought together banks of different nationalities with specialist knowledge of different markets. Unlike most consortia, though, they were not disbanded once their specific task was done.

CONSUMER

The ultimate beneficiary of industrialisation, and the only reason for any business to exist. The role of the consumer has changed in recent years. For as long as industry could scarcely supply enough goods and services to meet "consumer demand", it could afford to be cavalier about consumers' attitudes. Most of its attention then was focused on placating LABOUR and maximising production.

In the USA and Europe that situation changed sometime in the 1960s. Since then consumers have become more discerning. They have more choices, and manufacturers have to woo them.

Out of this grew (first) the consumer movement, led by pioneers like Ralph Nader. It set out to protect consumers themselves against commercial exploitation. It was followed by the green movement, which was also consumer-driven out of a concern for the damage that industry was causing to the environment.

Over time, the power structure within corporations has changed. Real power has shifted among the corporation's different constituencies: first it resided in the owner/manager, the original nineteenth century capitalist. Then it switched to labour with the growth of TRADE UNIONS and the post-war labour shortages in the West. Then it was the turn of the shareholder briefly to be "king" as CAPITAL again became the key factor of production. Now, perhaps, it is the turn of the environmentalist as the guardian of finite resources, another factor of production.

The consumer is not a moron; she is your wife.
David Ogilvy

CONSUMER DURABLES
CONSUMER goods (that is, goods on sale to the general public) that are designed to last and to be used over a period of time, such as dishwashers and televisions.

Because they are purchased infrequently, consumer durables have certain special properties.

- They are less sensitive to price than so-called fast-moving consumer goods (like toothpaste, chewing gum, etc). To some extent customers are prepared to wait until they can afford better quality.
- Manufacturers have to be looking continually for new markets to maintain sales; fast-moving consumer goods can maintain sales by sticking to the same market.
- They are more susceptible to downturns in the BUSINESS CYCLE. It is easier to tighten your belt by making do with an old washing machine than by giving up steak.

CONTRACT
An agreement in which one party agrees to supply goods or services to another in return for a "consideration", usually money. The agreement can be verbal but in business is usually written; even then there can be disagreement over what the agreement means. All contracts can be re-negotiated or broken, and some are void from the start because they involve illegal acts such as murder or INDUSTRIAL ESPIONAGE. The remedy for breach is usually damages; only in a very few cases – the sale of property in the UK,

for instance – can the buyer insist on "specific performance".

CONTROL

A word that is used in several different business contexts.

- A COMPANY which holds more than 50% of the voting rights of another company is said to control that company.
- Stock (or INVENTORY) control is a system of checking a company's inventory to see that it contains all that the records say it should.
- QUALITY CONTROL.
- Control systems are a combination of instruments used to check and operate automatically the controls of various production processes in industry. (See ROBOTICS.)
- In DIRECT MAIL, a control sample is used as a yardstick against which the success of future mail shots can be judged.

COPYRIGHT

The legal right of the creator of a literary, musical or artistic work to reproduce that work for gain, and to prevent anybody else from doing so. In many countries of the world copyright protection is weak; witness the plethora of pirated music and video cassettes that can be bought very cheaply in parts of the Far East.

The latest round of talks under the GATT is set upon tightening copyright protection in these places. It is a protection that will be greatly to the benefit of the USA and Europe at the expense of those countries whose individually creative work nobody else finds particularly interesting.

CORPORATE CULTURE

Every COMPANY, like every country, has its own distinctive culture. New employees often feel it, but find it hard to define. It is essentially the implicit or explicit priority that the company gives to different values. Some companies try to encapsulate it in their MISSION STATEMENT, and that can be helpful in giving employees a sense of identity. Some well-known companies have cultures that can be distilled into one-liners.

- **Hewlett Packard:** "Management by walking about."
- **Hanson:** "The shareholder is king."
- **Matsushita:** "Not for bread alone."
- **SAS (Scandinavian Airlines System):** "Flatten the pyramid."

A survey of business leaders conducted by the *Harvard Business Review* found wide cultural differences in managers' priorities. The following were the responses (the percentage of businessmen ticking each item) to the question: "What are the three most important factors for your organisation's success?"

Germany
Workforce skills	63
Problem solving	47
Management	44

Japan
Product development	54
Management	41
Product quality	36

USA
Customer service	52
Product quality	40
Technology	36

> *The only culture in this company is in the yoghurts in the canteen.*
> American executive

CORPORATE IDENTITY
The symbols by which a COMPANY is recognised; for example, the arches of McDonald's; the shell of Shell; the angle of the letters in Coca-Cola. These are valuable ASSETS, though nobody has yet tried to put them on a BALANCE SHEET.

COST

At its most basic, the amount of money that has to be paid in order to buy something. For example, "What is the cost of that doggy in the window?" From there accountants, economists and MANAGEMENT experts have stretched the use of this little word a long way.

● **Average cost.** The cost per unit of a business's output.

● **Carrying cost.** The cost of carrying (holding) stocks, machines and factories. The carrying cost is the amount that the money used to buy and maintain these ASSETS could earn if it were sitting in a bank.

● **CURRENT COST.**

● **DIRECT COST.**

● **FIXED COST.**

● **HISTORIC COST.**

● **INDIRECT COST.**

● **Marginal cost.** The cost of increasing a business's output by a single unit.

● **OPPORTUNITY COST.**

● **Overhead cost** (see OVERHEADS).

● **Production cost.** The total cost of getting a product to the factory gate ready for distribution.

● **REPLACEMENT COST.**

● **Transaction cost.** The cost attached to carrying out a transaction; for example, a bank's commission for buying foreign exchange.

● **Variable cost.** Costs that vary in proportion to the quantity of goods produced, such as lighting and heating and wages.

It's not cheaper things
That we want to possess,
But expensive things
That cost a lot less.
Anon

COST, INSURANCE, FREIGHT

Commonly known by its acronym CIF; part of a

trade CONTRACT which binds the exporter to pay not only the COST of getting the goods ready for transport, but also the cost of transporting them, and of insuring them while in transit. (See FREE ON BOARD.)

COTTAGE INDUSTRY

A business that could be run out of a cottage, like weaving, pottery and clock-making. But not all cottage industries are relics from before the INDUSTRIAL REVOLUTION. Modern HIGH-TECH businesses can also be cottage industries. In the Caribbean and on the west coast of Ireland, for example, there is a sizeable cottage industry in processing COMPUTER data, sent by satellite from the USA to these sources of cheap LABOUR.

COUNTERTRADE

A form of international BARTER in which goods and services are traded between countries for other goods and services rather than for cash. Countertrading has been a particularly popular way of trading with cash-starved eastern Europe in recent years.

Shortage of cash is not the only reason for countertrade deals. Members of OPEC have found countertrade deals a useful way of getting round OPEC-imposed production quotas.

Deals can become extremely complex: a multi-billion dollar deal between Turkey and the former Soviet Union, for instance, involved the export of huge quantities of Soviet natural gas to Turkey in return for a variety of Turkish products, ranging from fruit and textiles to engineering services. Such deals require somebody (a bank or government department) to act as a sort of clearing/payment house. In the above example, the Turkish gas CONSUMER has somehow to pay the Turkish engineering company. There is no way the engineer will accept payment in gas.

Anybody contemplating a countertrade deal would be well advised to get in touch with the specialist countertrade departments that now exist in many of the big international banks.

CREATIVE ACCOUNTING

A much-quoted story tells of an applicant for an accounting job who at his INTERVIEW was presented with a bundle of figures and asked to calculate the PROFIT. "Which profit did you have in mind?" he answered, and immediately got the job.

There are few absolutes in accounting; much of its art lies in interpretation. And within any interpretation there is scope for "creative accounting", something which makes the picture look prettier than it would otherwise. In the 1980s no go-go COMPANY could afford to be without a creative accountant or two.

CREDIT

A sum of money available for use. You can safely sell things to people whose credit is good. (See ACCEPTANCE CREDIT, DOCUMENTARY CREDIT.)

CREDIT GAP

The intellectual chasm between the interests of a seller in getting paid as quickly as possible, and the interests of a buyer in paying as late as possible.

CREDIT NOTE

An acknowledgement by a seller of goods or services that the buyer has been overcharged. The note gives the buyer the right to purchase goods in the future up to a stated amount.

CREDIT RATING

An assessment of the creditworthiness of a COM-PANY, an individual, or a debt instrument. In the USA credit rating is big business, and the practice is spreading rapidly to Europe. Two large firms dominate the business: Moody's and Standard & Poor's.

Credit-rating agencies supply (for a fee) analyses of creditworthiness for two types of customer.

- Traders who are about to do business with somebody for the first time and who need to get a feel for how much credit they can extend to that person or company, and for how long.

- Investors who want to have an assessment of the quality of a particular corporate debt instrument that they are thinking of buying.

Credit rating has come a long way from its origins as a private arrangement between a seller and a potential customer's bank, entered into with the full knowledge of the potential customer. There is now a secondary MARKET in credit ratings, and they can be passed around without the subject of the rating knowing anything about it. This practice has been controlled by legislation, and anybody now has the right to see any information about themselves held by a credit-rating agency. They also have the right to have it corrected if it is wrong.

CREDITOR

A COMPANY or individual to whom money is owed by a DEBTOR. The term "accounts payable" is used in the USA. (See also PREFERENTIAL CREDITOR.)

CRISIS MANAGEMENT

Most managers' regular jobs are interrupted occasionally by a crisis. Since such an event is an extreme of one sort or another, its consequences can also be extreme. So the proper handling of crises is of vital importance to a business. The classic case of crisis management occurred in 1990 when the Perrier bottled-water company withdrew 160m bottles from shops around the world after unacceptably high levels of benzene had been found in its water.

Learning about crisis management is a bit like learning the safety instructions in an aircraft before takeoff: you hope you will never need them, but you are not going to drop out of the class.

Here are a few widely recommended hints.

❏ Look out for advance warning of an impending crisis.

❏ Have a contingency plan and an alternative product or process ready.

❏ Speed of reaction is vital.

❏ Do not overreact.

❏ Watch out to see if competitors are trying to take advantage of your crisis.

❏ Be prepared to give up market share initially.

❏ Do not assume that everybody is hostile, and do not clam up.

❏ A crisis is the time to call upon GOODWILL that has been built up during the good times.

CROSS-RATE
The rate of exchange between two currencies calculated via a third currency, usually the dollar. Suppose there are 90 chetrums (the currency of Bhutan) to the dollar, and 900 pa'anga (the currency of Tonga) to the dollar. The cross-rate for Bhutanese travellers to Tonga is then 10 pa'angas to the chetrum.

CURRENT
Something which relates to the present.

CURRENT ACCOUNT
A type of bank account from which money can be withdrawn immediately and without the formal period of notice required by other forms of account. Also that part of a nation's trading account which shows the VALUE of its recent imports and exports of goods and services.

CURRENT ASSET
An asset that can be consumed by a business, now or in the near future. An example is RAW MATERIALS.

CURRENT COST
An accounting concept: the amount it would cost a COMPANY to buy one of its ASSETS today.

CUSTOM-MADE
Custom-made (or customized in the USA) is to

manufacturing as bespoke is to tailoring: something that is made to meet the particular specifications of an individual customer. This is a different order of things to the traditional manufacturing process, which makes something in the hope of subsequently finding a buyer.

CUSTOMER LOYALTY

The faithfulness of customers to a particular product or manufacturer. In some industries customer loyalty is very valuable, but beware: it can sometimes be mistaken for inertia. Consumers used to be loyal to their cars, buying the same manufacturer's models again and again. That has broken down in recent years with the disturbance in the industry caused by the Japanese.

D

DATABASE
A collection of information stored in a COMPUTER in an orderly way.

DATA PROCESSING
The placing and rearranging of information within a COMPUTER, and the subsequent transformation of that information by the computer's systems.

DEBENTURE
A type of BOND, issued by a corporation, whose documentation is held by trustees on behalf of the purchasers. Debentures usually have a charge on some specific ASSETS of the COMPANY. If the debenture holders are not repaid they can lay claim to those assets instead.

DEBUG
To remove the "bugs" from computers. Perhaps because computers are seen as dehumanising, the language of computers has become animated. Fructiferous brand names (like Apple and Apricot) abound, and there is an important piece of HARDWARE called a "mouse".

The idea that faults inside computer SOFTWARE are caused by little bugs is in the same vein. It is also apposite. The damage caused by a software fault can be on the same scale as that caused by ants eating through a giant sequoia tree.

DEBTOR
A COMPANY or individual who owes money to a CREDITOR. The term "accounts receivable" is used in the USA.

DEFAULT
The failure to repay a debt on time. Once a DEBTOR is in default, a lender has the right to follow legal processes to recover its loan.

DEFERRED TAX
The ACCOUNTS that a COMPANY prepares for its shareholders are not the same as those that it prepares for the tax inspector, and on which its tax

bill is assessed. There are certain things that accountants may net out of their calculation of PROFIT – such as transfers to reserves for future rainy days – which the tax inspector will want to add back for the calculation of taxable profit.

On the other hand, there are some things in the accountants' profit on which the tax inspector may postpone payment of tax. In such instances the company may set aside profits in its accounts to pay "deferred tax" at the later date on which it becomes due.

DEPRECIATION
Also known as amortisation. An amount that is charged against the profits of a COMPANY to take account of the fact that some of its fixed assets are wearing out and will have to be replaced. It allows accountants to spread the COST of things like plant and machinery over a number of years, instead of charging them all against the profit of the year in which they are bought.

Depreciation is probably the most inconsistently applied accounting standard in the world.
Center for International Financial Analysis and Research

DESIGN
A vital ingredient in the industrial process: the arranging of the appearance of a product. Design is more important to some industries than others. Obviously in fashion and jewellery it is the difference between success and failure. It is also crucial to the car, hotel and newspaper industries. With perfumes, the design of the bottle and of the packaging invariably costs several times as much as the perfume itself.

DESKTOP PUBLISHING
A specialised development of COMPUTER technology (closely associated with the US computer company Apple) that has turned almost every company into a publisher. With a personal

computer and a small number of software programs almost anybody can prepare a publication to the stage where it is in computer-ready form and fit for a specialist outside printer to print.

The power of desktop publishing (DTP) has resulted in a welter of in-house company publications, and the simultaneous destruction of any residual belief that the computer would create a "paperless society". The need now is for companies to concentrate on the purpose of their publications, and to stop wallowing in their ability to produce them.

DEVALUATION

A word that used to be on every businessman's lips in the days of fixed exchange rates: a sudden downward adjustment in the VALUE of a country's currency vis-à-vis another currency. Devaluations usually occurred at weekends amid much drama.

Under the Bretton Woods Agreement of 1944 exchange rates between currencies were fixed, and could only be changed by mutual agreement. But as countries' trade got out of balance (that is, they imported more than they exported) they forgot about mutual agreement and devalued to increase the local price of their imports. Once one country did this, other countries' trade then went out of balance. So they also devalued, and this cascade of "competitive devaluation" soon made the original one useless.

The Bretton Woods Agreement was abandoned in the early 1970s and exchange rates floated more freely. The European Monetary System, however, re-established a less rigid, semi-fixed exchange rate regime among the members of the EUROPEAN COMMUNITY.

DEVELOPMENT

See RESEARCH AND DEVELOPMENT.

DIFFERENTIATION

The process of making a product or service seem different from its competitors so that consumers ask specifically for it (by its brand name) rather than for

D

just anything that carries out the same function. Thus when shoppers ask for a jar of Maxwell House rather than for a jar of instant coffee, Maxwell House has successfully differentiated its product.

Differentiation can be established through any of the four Ps.

- **The product itself.**
- **The price.**
- **The promotion.** The way it is sold. A product sold as "non-fattening" may, for example, be no different from (and no less fattening than) a rival launched at a time when consumers were less weight-conscious. Nevertheless, its proclaimed slimming qualities will differentiate it in consumers' eyes.
- **The place.** Where it is sold. A cheese sold only through delicatessens, for example, can be priced higher than an identical cheese sold only through supermarkets. The cheese in the supermarket will, of course, be hoping to gain from a higher volume of sales.

DIGITAL
The representation of data by a series of digits. Thus a digital clock gives the time in the form of four digits (for example, 15.32), not as a pair of hands pointing at a face.

In a digital COMPUTER information is transmitted as a series of digits. In an analogue (or analog) computer some variable physical quality (such as electric voltage) represents the data. This allows analogue computers to function much quicker than digital ones.

DIRECT COST
A COST that is directly attributable to the production of a product; the cost of steel for a car manufacturer, for instance. The direct cost varies in direct proportion to the number of units produced, and is to be contrasted with OVERHEADS.

DIRECT MAIL
A method of selling goods and services by sending

catalogues, leaflets and order forms through the post. Sometimes known as "junk mail", there is a (false) belief that nobody reads direct mail on its way from the postman's bag to the bin. If it were so ineffective, would firms like Reader's Digest and Barclays Bank continue to use it so extensively?

DIRECTIVE

A key document in the process of EUROPEAN COMMUNITY law-making. Directives are issued by the European Commission to governments of member states "directing" them to introduce into their national legislation laws which the EC has passed.

These laws are passed after the Commission has produced several "draft directives", which are circulated for comment to the likes of industry associations and CONSUMER-protection groups. The Commission is obliged also to consider the opinion of the European Parliament on draft directives. Directives lose their draft status when the Council of Ministers has agreed to pass them into law.

DIRECTOR

A person appointed by shareholders to look after their interests in the MANAGEMENT of their COMPANY. The directors as a body constitute the BOARD of a company.

Company directors are restricted in what they can do: in general they cannot make contracts with the company, and they cannot take loans from the company (unless it is in the business of making loans, like a bank). Somebody who is declared BANKRUPT can only continue to be a director with the special permission of the court. If a company is deemed to have been trading when it was technically insolvent, directors can become personally liable for its debts. One of the few benefits for directors is that they are free effectively to fix their own remuneration.

The term director is also used more loosely, particularly in the USA, in the titles of senior management posts; for example, MARKETING director, personnel director. Such "directors" may well not have a seat on the board.

I emphasise the importance of details. You must perfect every fundamental of your business if you expect it to perform well.

Ray Kroc, founder of McDonald's

DISCOUNT

A reduction in the stated price of something. A discount can be offered for many reasons.

• A financial instrument may be sold at a discount to its face VALUE because the fixed rate of interest it pays is below the MARKET rate. When market interest rates are 10%, a $1,000 government bond with a 5% coupon (the rate of interest attached to it) will sell for $500; that is at a 50% discount.

• Vendors may give a discount for prompt payment in cash (a "cash discount"). Credit-card companies fought hard for years to prevent retailers which accepted their cards from giving cash discounts.

• Vendors often give a quantity discount which varies with the quantity of goods purchased. They can also give what is known as a trade discount to retailers or wholesalers in the same trade, as garment manufacturers do to dress shops, for example.

DISCRIMINATION

The practice of treating one set of things differently from another. Although economists talk of price discrimination (charging a different price for the same product in different markets), most talk of discrimination is of the sexual and racial kind. In developed countries it is illegal for a COMPANY to discriminate in any way on the grounds of a person's race or sex.

In the USA a number of companies have a policy of "positive discrimination". This entails employing more women and black people than is justified by their proportions in the general population in order to rectify past discrimination.

DISK DRIVE
That part of a COMPUTER which drives the machinery for recording and reading information stored on disks. (Disks are the magnetic flat plates inserted into slits in the front or side of computers. Those disks that can be bent easily are called floppy disks; those that cannot are called hard disks.)

DIVERSIFICATION
A currently unpopular corporate strategy that ensures a COMPANY does not have all its eggs in one basket. Diversification starts with the production of a product that has little to do with a company's existing product range; Bic, for example, the inventor of the ballpoint pen, diversified into the disposable razor business.

Many companies have come to grief by diversification. In *In Search of Excellence*, published in 1982, Tom Peters and Robert Waterman emphasised "the almost total absence of any rigorous support for very diversified business combinations". Yet at the time few paid attention.

Nowadays the popular strategy is to "stick to your knitting"; in other words do more of what you are good at. Those companies that have diversified successfully have usually done so in some way that was related to their existing markets. They have used the same distribution channels (for example, a company manufacturing handbags has diversified into making belts) or they have sold the same products into new markets (for example, a restaurant has diversified into providing a takeaway service).

DIVESTMENT
The opposite of DIVERSIFICATION; when companies get rid of certain businesses or operations that do not fit in with their mainstream strategy.

Paternalism is a word I rather bridle against because I think paternalism means that Daddy knows best, and I don't think that Daddy does.

Sir John Harvey-Jones when chairman of ICI, a company often accused of paternalism

DIVIDEND

The amount of a COMPANY's annual PROFIT that is set aside for the company's shareholders, known affectionately as the "divi". A company may decide to pay an "interim dividend" in the middle of the financial year as a sort of advance on the full-year payment.

When a company has had a good year then the dividend payment should be high, and vice versa, but too often things do not work out like that. Shareholders expect dividends to increase every year without fail, rather like an indexed interest payment. Companies dare not frustrate the expectations of these shareholders turned bondholders for fear of the effect they might have on their SHARE price.

Shares are sometimes sold on the STOCKMARKET "cum dividend", meaning that the price for the share includes the company's next dividend payment (which has probably been announced but not yet paid).

(See also INTEREST COVER.)

DOCUMENTARY CREDIT

A method of financing trade in which importers of goods get credit from a bank on the basis of documents which prove that the goods are rightly theirs. This enables them to pay the vendors of the goods before they are able to sell them on themselves. Documentary credits have been assisted by the growth of FAX machines and international courier services, both of which enable documents to travel so much faster than goods.

DOUBLE-ENTRY

The fundamental principle of BOOK-KEEPING, and therefore of accounting, that every entry in a

COMPANY's books has an equal and opposite counterpart. Every transaction that a company effects creates an asset on one side of the ledger, and an equal and opposite liability on the other.

This duality of business transactions means that a company's books must always balance; that is, the monetary VALUE of each side of the ledger must be equal. This is the origin of the expression "BALANCE SHEET". Double-entry book-keeping has been around for centuries; its early development is usually attributed to fourteenth-century Italians.

DOUBLE-TAXATION AGREEMENT

When companies start to trade in a number of countries they can find themselves liable to tax in more than one jurisdiction. A company will normally be liable to domestic tax on all its world-wide PROFIT, no matter where it arises. It may also be liable to tax on that same profit in the country in which it arises.

To help companies avoid thus being taxed twice on the same profit in two different places, many pairs of countries have so-called double-taxation agreements between themselves. These are often very complicated and deal with much more than company profits; they may include, for example, provisions to avoid the double taxation of income, dividends or interest payments. The agreements normally allow companies which have been taxed on profits in the country where they arose to deduct those taxes from their tax bill in their country of residence. Moreover, when there is no double-taxation agreement, companies can often treat the tax paid abroad as a deductible expense when calculating their domestic taxable profit.

DOUBTFUL DEBT

A COMPANY's debts are either good, bad or doubt-ful. They are good if they still fall within the agreed repayment period, or within the period (30, 60 or 90 days) that is standard for the industry. If they are still unpaid beyond that period they become doubtful. Companies then put aside

an amount of their PROFIT against the possibility
that the debt (which is in their books as an asset)
will not be repaid.

Some companies go through each individual
doubtful debt and assess the likelihood of its
being repaid. Others simply set aside a percentage (based on industry experience) of all their
doubtful debts.

A debt becomes bad when the person or company who owes it goes BANKRUPT, or has no possibility of repaying. The company then has to
"write off" the debt, and take the whole amount
of it out of its profits.

DOWNMARKET
A MARKETING term which assumes that markets
have a top and a bottom, and that products continually move "UPMARKET" towards the top, or
"downmarket" towards the bottom.

It is not always clear what scale this top and
bottom are on: is it the price of the product; the
social class of the buyer; or the exclusivity of the
product? Is a basic Rolls-Royce car a downmarket
product? Is every shop in Gstaad or Vail upmarket?

DTP
See DESKTOP PUBLISHING.

DUTCH AUCTION
An auction in which the auctioneer starts by asking a high price which is gradually lowered until
a buyer is found. The wonderful Dutch flower
auctions are organised in this way. It is the opposite of most auctions held more than 50 miles
from Amsterdam. In a non-Dutch auction it is the
last bidder who gets the lot on sale; in a Dutch
auction the first bidder gets it.

DUTIES
Taxes on particular goods or services. Duties are
roughly divided into two.

• **Import duties.** Imposed on goods brought

into a country (often called tariffs). The so-called duty-free shops found at airports and border posts are a misnomer. The prices of goods sold there (alcohol, tobacco, watches, perfume, and so on) are far higher than they would be if there were no duty on them whatsoever.

- **Excise duties.** Imposed on goods or services produced within the country that is levying the tax.

Excise duties are popularly imposed on alcohol, tobacco and petrol. There are also things called stamp duties which are paid when shares or property are sold; and death duties, which are imposed on the property of the recently deceased.

E

EC
See EUROPEAN COMMUNITY.

ECONOMIC AND MONETARY UNION
The process of integrating the currencies and
monetary policies of the 12 member states of the
EUROPEAN COMMUNITY. Economic and monetary
union (EMU) began in the early 1970s with something called "the snake", a managed EXCHANGE-
RATE system which aimed to limit fluctuations
between EC currencies.

The snake effectively died in 1976, but three
years later a new European Monetary System
(EMS) was born. It was based on something called
the EUROPEAN CURRENCY UNIT (ecu).

In the Exchange-Rate Mechanism (ERM) of the
EMS, European currencies can fluctuate within a
given percentage of their rate against the ecu.
Should they threaten to break outside the percentage band, then central banks agree to inter-
vene, buying or selling currencies to adjust the
rates. Should that not be enough, then governments have to adjust interest rates, or other internal economic variables.

By the late 1980s continental Europe was keen
to take the process of monetary union further. At
a meeting in Maastricht at the end of 1991 the
Community provisionally agreed to take a number of steps.

- **1991–94.** Completion of the first stage of EMU,
with greater integration of EC monetary and economic policies. All member states will come within the narrow band of the ERM.
- **January 1st 1994.** The second stage of EMU
begins. The composition of the basket of currencies in the ecu is frozen, and a European Monetary Institute (EMI) is set up to co-ordinate
member states' monetary policy.
- **End-1996.** A report on progress will show
how far member states' economies have
converged in terms of inflation, interest rates and
budget deficits. On the basis of this report it will
be decided how to move to the third stage of

EMU, in which member states will share a single currency and a single European central bank.

The widening of the exchange rate bands after the near collapse of the ERM in 1993 were a big setback for EMU.

ECONOMIES OF SCALE
The average COST of a manufactured unit decreases when more units are manufactured. For example, if it costs $X to make ten cars, it costs much less than $2X to make 20 cars because much of the expense involved in making the first ten does not have to be repeated to make another ten. Such "economies of scale" lie behind all MASS PRODUCTION, and help to make highly sophisticated products available to many.

There are limits to economies of scale. The bigger a plant becomes the more unmanageable it is. The cost of this unmanageability eventually outweighs the benefits from economies of scale. The president of Motorola, the American electronics firm, once said: "When a plant starts to edge towards 1,500 people, somehow, like magic, things start to go wrong."

ECU
See EUROPEAN CURRENCY UNIT.

EEA
See EUROPEAN ECONOMIC AREA.

EFTA
See EUROPEAN FREE TRADE ASSOCIATION.

EGM
See EXTRAORDINARY GENERAL MEETING.

EIB
See EUROPEAN INVESTMENT BANK.

ELECTRONIC MAIL
The transmission of electronic "letters" from one COMPUTER to another. The computers have to be

linked to telecommunications systems by means of a MODEM which translates computer signals into telecom signals. On arrival at their destination the signals are translated back into computerese by another modem.

The growth in electronic mail has been less than its potential once suggested it might be. It has certainly not put paper mills out of business. People like to see a "hard copy" of information that they receive: the great majority of electronic messages get printed on to paper upon receipt.

EMBARGO
A ban on something: for example, a government-imposed ban on trading with a particular country; for example, with Iraq after it invaded Kuwait.

An embargo can also be a ban imposed on the publishing of a sensitive piece of news. COMPANY press releases sent out to newspapers and magazines sometimes carry a notice at the top saying "Embargoed until 00.00 hours on such-and-such date". The company then trusts the journalists not to print the information until after that time.

EMPLOYEE SHARE OPTION
A method whereby employees in a COMPANY are given an option to buy shares in that company at some future date. The price at which they can exercise the option is below the MARKET price.

Traditionally share options were granted to directors and senior managers, partly as a reward and partly in order to increase their commitment to the company. Nowadays options are being granted to more lowly employees, often to entice people with particular skills into a company. They have not, however, been so widespread as materially to bridge the gap between those people who work for a corporation and those who own it.

EMPLOYMENT AGENCIES
PUBLIC-SECTOR and PRIVATE-SECTOR bodies that attempt to match the supply of LABOUR with the demand. Some agencies specialise in supplying particular industries or skills; others in supplying

temporary replacements ("temps") for jobs that are only vacant for a while. Employment agents for top managers are called "headhunters".

EMPLOYMENT CONTRACT
The formal agreement between an employer and an employee laying down the terms and conditions of his or her employment in the COMPANY. In most developed countries it is now illegal to discriminate between employees; they must have the same CONTRACT for the same work.

EMS
See under ECONOMIC AND MONETARY UNION.

EMU
See ECONOMIC AND MONETARY UNION.

ENTERPRISE
Either a business organisation (as in "state enterprise"); or an economic system in which people are free to do business more or less as they wish (as in "free enterprise"); or the quality exemplified by the risk-taking businessman (as in "Richard Branson showed great enterprise in setting up Virgin Airlines" or "Sam Walton showed great enterprise in setting up Wal-Mart Stores").

Whichever it is, successful economies cannot do without it.

I reckon one entrepreneur can recognise another at 300 yards on a misty day.
Sir Peter Parker, a former chairman of British Rail

ENVIRONMENTAL AUDIT
An attempt to use the checks and balances of auditing to assess the CONTROL that a COMPANY has over its impact on the environment. The International Chamber of Commerce (ICC) defines an environmental audit as "a MANAGEMENT tool comprising a systematic, documented, periodic and objective evaluation of how well environmental organisation,

---

management and equipment are performing".

The idea is a fairly new one, born out of "green consciousness", though some companies (like Shell Oil) have been carrying out environmental audits for over a decade. Shell says that a successful environmental audit requires the following.

- Full management commitment.
- Careful selection of the audit team to ensure objectivity.
- Well-defined systematic procedures.
- The preparation of written reports.
- Quality assurance.
- Follow-up.

EQUAL OPPORTUNITIES

The idea that all men and women should have an equal opportunity to climb the corporate ladder. Although many countries have legislation to enforce equal opportunities, there are still inequalities between men and women in the workforce.

At the shopfloor level women have used equal opportunities legislation to get the same rate of pay for the same job as men, and for the right to work the same (more highly paid) overtime as men. (In some countries, for instance, it has long been illegal for women to work at night.)

At more senior management levels women have been held back by the so-called "glass ceiling". Nobody can yet say that women and men have an equal opportunity to be chief executive of General Motors.

EQUITY

The financial interest of shareholders in their COMPANY. In accounting terms that means the VALUE of the company's ASSETS minus its LIABILITIES. On a BALANCE SHEET this is referred to as "shareholders' funds". This equity is divided "equitably" among shareholders according to the number of shares they hold.

ERM

See under ECONOMIC AND MONETARY UNION.

EUROMARKET

Financial markets in currencies held outside the country that issued them, usually dollars held outside the USA or Deutschemarks held outside Germany, called Eurodollars and EuroDeutschemarks respectively.

These currencies are held with banks in financial centres like London, Luxembourg, Hong Kong and the Cayman Islands, where there are fewer regulations than in the USA or Germany. (So banks there can pay better rates for deposits since regulation always has a COST.)

Another advantage to these markets is that there is less chance of the deposits being frozen for political reasons, as has occurred on occasion to foreign deposits in the USA.

EUROPEAN COMMUNITY

The 12 countries of Western Europe that have signed the Treaty of Rome pledging themselves to close co-operation with each other. They are:

• **Belgium, France, Italy, Luxembourg, the Netherlands and West Germany**, the original six that signed the treaty on March 25th 1957;
• **Denmark, Ireland and the UK** (which joined in 1973);
• **Greece** (1981);
• **Portugal and Spain** (1986).

There were originally three communities: the EEC, the European Economic Community; the ECSC, the European Coal and Steel Community; and EURATOM, which is the European Atomic Energy Community. In 1967 the three were merged into the single European Community.

The European Community (EC) has three main organs.

1 The European Commission. Based in Brussels it drafts policies by publishing directives, and acts as the civil service to the Community. (See DIRECTIVE.)
2 The Council of Ministers. In practice a

E

*Where there is no big vision, the people
will perish.*

Jean Monnet, founder of the EC

number of committees made up of one minister
per member state. They pass (or do not pass) the
directives proposed by the Commission. Directives concerned with agriculture, for example,
will be considered by a council consisting of the
agriculture ministers of the 12 member states.

3 The European Parliament. Meets mostly in
Strasbourg and is consulted on all proposals that
come from the Commission. Members of the
European Parliament are directly elected by constituencies throughout the Community.

The Community's most powerful influence is economic, through its gradual creation of a SINGLE
MARKET among the 340m inhabitants of the 12
member states. In such a market, it is the inten-
tion that goods, capital and LABOUR should move
as freely as if the Twelve were one.

*By 1995 Rhône-Poulenc wants two tiers of its
managers to become "jeunes sans frontières",
young people who can forget the notion of
nationality and help build a truly global company.*

Company statement

EUROPEAN CURRENCY UNIT

The denomination that dedicated Europeans
hope will become a single European currency,
accepted in shops from Bari to Aberdeen, and
from Berlin to Lisbon.

The European currency unit (ecu) was originally a technical creation that existed only on paper.
It was a theoretical basket of European currencies
– a few pence added to a few francs plus a bit of
a Deutschemark, and so on – the amount of each
currency in the basket determined by the size of
the economy that issued it. Countries that partici-
pated in the European Monetary System then set
their EXCHANGE RATE in terms of this ecu.

Gradually the ecu began to be used in commercial transactions. The European Commission denominates its invoices in ecus; some banks offer ecu deposits and ecu loans; and, for a short while, shops in part of Luxembourg quoted all their prices in ecus.

EUROPEAN ECONOMIC AREA

European Economic Area (EEA) is a term used to describe the 19 countries of the EUROPEAN COMMUNITY and the seven which belong to the EUROPEAN FREE TRADE ASSOCIATION. In October 1991 these two blocs agreed to set up a common market embracing all their members. Its main features were to be as follows.

• Free movement of goods within the area.
• Special arrangements covering food, fish, energy, coal and steel.
• EFTA to adopt EC rules on company law, consumer protection, education, the environment, R&D, and social policy.
• EFTA to adopt EC rules on competition, abuse of a dominant position, public procurement, mergers and state aid.
• An independent court to handle EEA disputes on competition policy.
• Mutual recognition of qualifications, and freedom to live and work anywhere in the area.
• Switzerland to have an extra five years to remove its tight laws on immigration.
• The freeing of capital movements, although controls will remain on some direct investment in EFTA and on some foreign purchases of EFTA real estate.
• EFTA countries to be free to stay outside the EC's common agricultural policy (CAP).

But progress towards the EEA has been slower than anticipated.

EUROPEAN FREE TRADE ASSOCIATION

A European trading bloc consisting of Austria, Finland, Iceland, Liechtenstein, Norway, Sweden and Switzerland. The headquarters of the

European Free Trade Association (EFTA) are in Geneva. Denmark, Portugal and the UK were all members of EFTA until they were given a chance to join the EC.

EFTA is less ambitious than the EC. It has removed tariffs and quotas on goods moving from one member state to another, but each member retains its own tariffs against third countries' imports. The EC, on the other hand, has harmonised its tariffs against non-EC countries.

Much of the external trade of the two European communities (EFTA and the EC) is with each other, and there have been a number of treaties reducing trade barriers between them. Several EFTA members have indicated that they would like to join the EC and as time goes by the two blocs will in any case become closer, melding into a 19-nation unit that has already been christened the EUROPEAN ECONOMIC AREA.

EUROPEAN INVESTMENT BANK

The European Investment Bank (EIB) was created by the Treaty of Rome, the treaty which also established the EUROPEAN COMMUNITY. The EIB is a development bank which uses its good reputation to borrow cheaply on various international financial markets, and then lends to borrowers within the EC and its associate member states (countries like Cyprus and Malta that are at a half-way stage towards full membership). EIB loans are long-term and have maturities of 7–12 years.

The bank has certain priority areas in its lending.

- Depressed regions, like most of Portugal and large parts of Ireland.
- The development of European technology.
- Joint infrastructure projects (like the Channel Tunnel) involving more than one member state.

EXCHANGE CONTROL

Government rules on the amount of its currency that can be taken out of a country or, in some instances, that can be brought in. The most familiar sort of exchange CONTROL is imposed on travellers at their entry or exit from certain countries. The more significant form of exchange control, however, is imposed on companies, and limits their ability to finance trade or investment abroad with their own currency. The aim of exchange controls is to support the EXCHANGE RATE (that is the price) of a nation's currency by limiting the sale of it.

In recent years governments have used interest rates rather than exchange controls as the main economic tool for adjusting exchange rates. Exchange controls went out of fashion for several reasons.

• The EUROMARKET grew as a location in which to keep currencies OFFSHORE. These currencies never came home and could be used abroad whenever their owners wanted, regardless of exchange controls.
• The free-market economics espoused by Margaret Thatcher and Ronald Reagan was philosophically opposed to exchange controls. The UK abolished virtually all its (once extensive) exchange controls in 1979, the year that Mrs Thatcher came into office.
• The development of the EUROPEAN COMMUNITY depended on the removal of barriers to the free flow of capital among EC member states. This implied the complete removal of exchange controls, although some member states (like France and Italy) have been slow to comply with EC directives on this.

When a currency's only friends are central bankers, it is heading for a fall.
The Economist

EXCHANGE RATE
The price at which one currency can be exchanged for another. The basic price for most currencies is expressed in dollars.

E

Exchange rates come in various forms.

- **Fixed rate.** Governments fix the rate against something else: the price of gold, the dollar, or the ecu, for example. When it has to change the rate, a government does so either by a devaluation (increasing the amount of currency per dollar, ounce of gold, or whatever); or by a revaluation (decreasing the amount of currency per unit).
- **Floating rate.** Governments allow their currency to find its own level according to demand in the foreign-exchange markets.
- **Forward rate.** The exchange rate today for delivery of a currency at some future date. It removes risk for companies to buy currencies in the "forward MARKET" when they know that they have to pay large foreign-currency bills in the future. Forward rates are usually expressed as a premium (or DISCOUNT) on the spot rate.
- **Spot rate.** The exchange rate for immediate delivery of a currency: "on the spot", as opposed to "forward". Will a currency that is too forward find itself on the spot?
- **Two-tier rate.** Some countries (like South Africa) have a fixed rate for certain types of transaction (like trade) and a different rate for all other transactions.
- **Unofficial rate.** In countries with a fixed rate there is frequently an illegal black market where currency is bought and sold freely. The price in the black market is called the unofficial rate.

Executive: an ulcer with authority.
Fred Allen

EXPATRIATE
A favourite figure in literature (because so many writers are themselves expatriates?); the manager or skilled worker who is a foreigner in the country where he or she is working and living. Strictly speaking an expatriate is sent abroad by his or

her employer for a relatively short term, but that definition has been stretched to suit modern times. Expatriates nowadays may well be employed by the local SUBSIDIARY of the COMPANY that sent them abroad, or indeed by a local company itself, for life.

Expatriates who are sent to live in unappealing places expect to get a number of generous perks (see FRINGE BENEFITS) to compensate; for example, regular free trips back home, school fees for their children, and various cost-of-living allowances. In general, the less pleasant the destination, the more perks the employee gets. One large firm of accountants reckons it costs three times as much to send a person to Moscow as it does to send them to Paris.

EXPORT CREDIT AGENCY

A government (or quasi-government) agency which does one or both of two things.

• Lends money to foreign buyers to buy goods from the country in which the agency is based. When the country is keen to boost exports these loans are offered at subsidised rates.
• Guarantees loans from banks to the domestic exporter. Such loans finance the transaction until the exporter is paid.

The USA's export credit agency is called Ex-Im Bank, France's is Coface, Germany's is Hermes and the UK's is the Export Credits Guarantee Department (ECGD). To prevent these agencies from cut-throat COMPETITION, countries have agreed on what are called "consensus rates". These are interest rates that define the extent to which agencies can subsidise loans to purchase their own country's exports.

If we take care of our imports, our exports will take care of themselves.
Anon

E

EXPORT CREDIT INSURANCE
A form of insurance taken out by exporters to cover their risk between the time that they ship goods to a customer and the time that they receive payment for the goods. Such insurance can be obtained from either an EXPORT CREDIT AGENCY in the form of a guarantee to a bank for loans given to the exporter; or (to a more limited extent) private insurance companies which, for a fee, will cover the risk of non-payment.

EXPORT LICENCE
A document obtained from an official body allowing the export of goods which it is otherwise forbidden to take out of a country. Most countries require such licences for the export of antiques, works of art and military equipment, or for any sort of equipment that may be used for military purposes.

EXTRAORDINARY GENERAL MEETING
As its name suggests, an extraordinary general meeting (EGM) is an out-of-the-ordinary meeting of a COMPANY's shareholders to consider things that cannot wait until the next annual general meeting (see AGM). The circumstances under which an EGM can be called, and the procedures to be followed, are usually laid down in the company's articles of association. If not, then company law determines the procedures.

The sort of thing that an EGM might be called upon to consider could be a takeover bid; a proposed restructuring of the company's EQUITY; or shenanigans among the company's managers.

EXTRAORDINARY ITEM
This is exactly what it says: an item in a COMPANY's ACCOUNTS that is out of the ordinary. What constitutes extraordinary, however, is not so simple. By and large extraordinary items are revenues and expenses that do not come from the normal course of a company's operations, and should therefore be shown BELOW-THE-LINE in the accounts, that is after the key figure of net PROFIT

has been calculated. That creates a great temptation for companies to call all revenue items ordinary, and all expenditure items extraordinary.

UK companies go in for the extraordinary to an extraordinary degree: over half of one sample had extraordinary items in their 1989 accounts, compared with less than 10% in a comparable sample of US companies. The UK accounting profession is trying to tighten up on the uses and abuses of extraordinary items in accounts. It is introducing rules which will mean that all items are ordinary unless they display "a high degree of abnormality". Whether that is a helpful clarification remains to be seen.

F

FACTORING

The practice of subcontracting to someone else (called the factor, and usually a financial COMPANY) the business of collecting money due on a company's invoices. There are two main reasons for factoring.

- The company is too small for it to be efficient to run its own sales ledger (see BOOK-KEEPING). In this case the factor will be paid a fee and will do everything from raising an invoice to chasing poor payers.
- The company is in need of cash and wants to accelerate payments due to it. In this case the factor "buys" the company's unpaid invoices at a DISCOUNT, and then sets about collecting the money itself. This is a one-off operation, and the factor's fee is anything that it can collect above the discounted amount it paid for the invoices.

In this second type of factoring (sometimes known as invoice discounting) the company may not wish it to be known that it has sold its invoices (and is therefore in need of cash). In such cases the factor may continue to send out claims for payment in the company's name.

FACTORY

Originally a trading post in far-flung parts of the British Empire – like India and Canada – that was run by a "factor" (that is, an AGENT from Europe employed by the earliest large COMPANY, the East India Company, to run its trading posts). Factories, of course, are also places that use the economist's three "factors of production": LABOUR, land and CAPITAL.

The word factory came to conjure up images of chimneys, "satanic mills" and the exploitation of labour. This led to the various Factory Acts passed in the UK and the USA in the nineteenth century to protect the health and safety of factory workers.

FAST TRACK

A special career path within an organisation, designed for particularly able people who are **not** going to wait around until they have climbed all the steps of a normal career ladder to the top. The disadvantage of such a system is that it alienates those slower mortals who may, in the end, be the more able top managers.

FAX

The facsimile machine, perhaps the most commercially significant invention to come out of the last 40 years of the twentieth century. Known affectionately by its diminutive name, the facsimile machine scans a document of words or images and transmits them down telephone lines to another machine which converts the messages into a "facsimile" copy of the original document. At the moment that image is only reproduced in black and white, but it will not be long before colour images can be transmitted too.

The fax has reinvented that great nineteenth-century service without which no Victorian novelist's plot would have got far: fast mail delivery. It is estimated that more than half the telephone calls between New York and Japan are now fax calls. The machine has become so popular that it has bred "junk" fax: unsolicited messages transmitted much as junk mail is sent. If left on the specially sensitive fax paper, however, these messages can fade in as little as three months. Lawyers and all careful business people always take photocopies.

Japanese companies have obtained an extraordinarily high share of the world's MARKET for facsimile machines. That was in part due to a strategy of remorseless price cutting which created greater demand. That in turn enabled the manufacturers to make ECONOMIES OF SCALE, and to cut prices further.

To me success can only be achieved through repeated failure and introspection. In fact, success represents the 1% of your work which results from the 99% that is called failure.
Soichiro Honda, founder of Honda

FDI
See FOREIGN DIRECT INVESTMENT.

FIFO
See FIRST IN, FIRST OUT.

FINANCIAL YEAR
The 12-month period for which a COMPANY draws up its annual ACCOUNTS. This is not necessarily the calendar year January 1st–December 31st. Many companies close their financial year at the end of March, which is just as well. If all companies chose the calendar year auditors would be rushed off their feet in January, February and March, and idle for the rest of the year.

Some companies choose more peculiar financial years (to the end of September, for example) for sound commercial reasons. Agricultural businesses may want their financial years to end when a seasonal harvest has been gathered and sold. Other companies sometimes have financial years that last longer than 12 months. Accounts can be drawn up for a 15-month period if, for example, a company wants to change the end of its financial year from September 30th to December 31st. The reasons for doing this may be no more substantial than a desire to confuse shareholders by spoiling comparisons between one period and the next.

FIRING
Also known as sacking. The following guidelines should be adopted.

❏ All dismissals must be in accordance with employment law.
❏ If a disciplinary procedure exists ensure it is adhered to.
❏ Allow employees to state their case.
❏ Investigate thoroughly before making a decision.
❏ In cases of alleged gross misconduct suspend on full pay during investigation.
❏ Do not lose your temper; hasty words can be

construed as a dismissal when none was intended.
❑ Keep written records of all stages of the procedure.

He was fired with enthusiasm because he wasn't fired with enthusiasm.

Anon

FIRST IN, FIRST OUT

Commonly known by its acronym FIFO; a method of valuing stock-in-trade for accounting purposes. A COMPANY has a sizeable stock of identical inputs to be used in production. They have been purchased at different times and at different prices. Are the most recent purchases being used up first, or the oldest? Since they are identical, you cannot tell merely by looking at them.

FIFO assumes that the oldest (probably those bought at the lowest price) are used up first, and is the opposite of LIFO (LAST IN, FIRST OUT). FILO (first in, last out) is not a method of valuing stock; it is a description of the daily arrival and departure of the good leader.

FIXED ASSET

An asset that remains in the business over time and is not merely being processed on its way from a supplier to a CONSUMER. Fixed ASSETS include things like office buildings, factories and land, but they are not necessarily fixed to the ground. Portable computers are fixed assets to anybody but a portable-computer manufacturer. The shares that a COMPANY owns in subsidiaries or associated companies are also fixed assets.

FIXED COST

A COST that does not vary with the amount of goods or services produced (the opposite of variable cost). Fixed costs are items like rent and bank interest: items that have to be paid regardless of whether anything at all is produced or sold.

F

Philosophically there are no costs that are fixed in the long term, because in the long term, to quote one author, "any productive process is optional".

FLEXITIME
A schedule of work that allows employees to choose their own working hours around a "core time" at the middle of the day. Under this system employees are required to work, say, eight hours a day, and to be working between, say, 11.00 and 15.00. They can then choose whether they work from 07.00 to 15.00, or from 11.00 to 19.00, or any eight hours between.

Flexitime only works where employees are involved in individual tasks, like architecture or door-to-door selling. It cannot be applied to jobs where continuous teamwork is required, or where (like teaching) the customer is only present within certain hours.

FLOATING CHARGE
A CHARGE that can be applied across all a COMPANY's ASSETS. An unpaid CREDITOR with a floating charge has a right to claim any of the company's assets. A creditor with a fixed charge, on the other hand, has a right only to those assets (such as a building) that are specifically mentioned in the charge.

FLOATING-RATE NOTE
A debt instrument popular in the Euromarkets on which the interest rate is adjusted periodically to take account of changing MARKET conditions. The interest rate of floating-rate notes (FRNs) is often expressed with reference to some variable base point, frequently LIBOR (the London interbank offered rate), a variable rate that banks in London offer to pay to each other for foreign currency deposits.

FLOPPY DISK
The disk that is inserted into computers in order to give them greater storage capacity, or the ability to perform new tricks. In fact floppy disk is fast becoming a misnomer. Disks used to flop

and be 5¼ inches in diameter, but the standard size for the industry is changing. More and more disks are 3½ inches across, and they are "hard" not floppy.

FLOW OF FUNDS

A synonym for CASH FLOW. In some countries companies are required to publish a third statement in their annual ACCOUNTS, alongside their PROFIT AND LOSS ACCOUNT and their BALANCE SHEET. This is to show the flow of funds in and out of the company during an accounting period.

In the USA this third statement is known as the Funds Flow Statement. In the UK it is known as the Source and Use of Funds.

FOB

See FREE ON BOARD.

FOREIGN DIRECT INVESTMENT

The investment by residents of one country in the industries of another, either through the ACQUISITION of a stake of more than 10% of a COMPANY, or by the setting up of a GREENFIELD SITE. Stakes of less than 10% are defined as PORTFOLIO investment. Many nations remain ambivalent about foreign direct investment (FDI), not wanting to see their domestic industries taken over and controlled by foreigners.

The Americans were the first to invest heavily overseas after the second world war, and they were heavily criticised for it in *Le Défi Americain*, a controversial book written by a Frenchman, Jean-Jacques Servan-Schreiber. Nowadays FDI is seen more as the natural way of a global world. Many countries court it assiduously.

The Japanese have taken over from the Americans and the Europeans (particularly the Dutch and the British) as the biggest foreign direct investors around the world. The wheel has turned full circle for the Americans who have been very hostile to Japanese purchases of what have been seen as great US ASSETS (like the Rockefeller Center and the CBS recording company). Heavy Japanese investment in the UK has been seen by other Europeans as a Trojan horse for the unwelcome Japanese to get inside the EUROPEAN COMMUNITY.

If trade is the child, FDI is the adult. Japanese companies' VCR plants in Europe reduce the need to ship VCRs from plants in Japan. FDI brings nations into closer touch than does long-distance trade. Japanese managers at VCR factories in Europe rub shoulders with Europeans every day. This integrates cultures in a way that nobody yet fully understands. In the future, international commercial relations are going to be shaped much more by FDI than they are by trade.

FOREIGN INVESTMENT
Investment by one country in the SECURITIES or ASSETS of another country. This includes the purchase of large chunks of industrial companies (see FOREIGN DIRECT INVESTMENT) as well as the purchase of property and of small amounts of securities.

The flows of foreign investment around the world are increasing dramatically. In one sense foreign investment is the mirror image of a CURRENT ACCOUNT surplus. If a country (like Japan) continually exports more than it imports then, in its balance of payments, its surplus must be "balanced" by a corresponding outflow of CAPITAL.

FORTUNE 500
The annual listing by *Fortune*, the US business magazine, of the 500 largest corporations in the USA. The magazine also publishes an annual list of the 500 largest corporations outside the USA. Companies jealously watch their positions in these rankings, the most prestigious of many. All rankings, however, suffer from a number of failings.

• It is hard to decide what measure of size to use: sales/TURNOVER, total ASSETS, PROFIT, or MARKET capitalisation (what a company is worth). All of these have been used in at least one reputable listing. (*Fortune* uses sales.)
• They all have drawbacks. For example, using

sales as a yardstick always pushes to the top those companies dealing in commodity-like products (such as oil or grain). Their margins are small, and to make a reasonable business they have to have relatively huge turnovers.

• Some yardsticks cannot cope with certain industries. Sales figures, for instance, have little meaning for financial institutions. Banks are usually compared in terms of total assets. But total assets have little meaning for service companies, like software firms or firms of accountants. They have few assets of the type that appear on balance sheets.

• By highlighting size, the listings promote the idea that big is beautiful and that size is all that matters. Companies are pushed to emphasise quantity at the expense of quality, be it of sales, profits, assets, or whatever.

FORWARD CONTRACT

A CONTRACT between two companies for the delivery of specified goods or currency at some specified time in the future and for a specified price. A forward contract differs from a FUTURES contract in that it is not entered into primarily to create a tradeable instrument.

Forward contracts shift various risks from a buyer to a seller and vice versa; for example, the danger that INFLATION or EXCHANGE-RATE fluctuations will erode the VALUE of the contract, or that something (like a STRIKE) will prevent the company from delivering as promised.

FRANCHISE

A popular way for a manufacturer or service COMPANY to distribute its goods or services widely without making all the necessary CAPITAL investment itself. Some famous franchise operations include McDonald's restaurants and Benetton clothes shops.

A franchisor usually gives a licence to a franchisee for a certain fee which is frequently based on the franchisee's turnover. The licence gives the franchisee the exclusive right to sell the franchisor's goods or services in a particular area. In return the franchisee has to meet certain standards demanded by the franchisor, and also has to buy supplies only from the franchisor. Luciano Benetton says he gives franchises not necessarily to people with merchandising experience, but to people with "the right spirit". He teaches them merchandising the Benetton way.

FREE ON BOARD

A term attached to a price quotation given by an exporter. Free on board (FOB) means that the exporter undertakes, for that price, to deliver the goods to the buyer's chosen method of transport, usually a ship.

The French expression is *franco à bord* and it has various modifications.

- **Franco frontier.** Free delivery to the border of the exporter's country.
- **Franco quai.** Free as far as the quay beside the ship that is to transport the goods.
- **Franco wagon.** Free as far as the train that is to carry the goods.

FREE-TRADE ZONE

Areas where foreign goods are allowed to come and go free from tariffs and other barriers to trade. Often near seaports and airports, free-trade zones typically consist of a number of industrial plants where imported goods are processed before being re-exported. Since the imports never technically enter the country where the free-trade zone is located, they do not have to go through elaborate (and expensive) customs procedures. Free-trade zones are suitable for processes such as CMT (cut, make and trim), in which imported fabric is made into garments for re-export.

Free trade, one of the greatest blessings which a government can confer on a people, is in almost every country unpopular.
Lord Macaulay

FRINGE BENEFITS

Also known as perks, these are rewards given to
employees on top of their normal wages or
salaries. They include things like pensions, private health insurance, cars, sports facilities, lun-
cheon vouchers, low-interest loans and (less
obviously) pay for time not worked; during holidays, sickness or TRAINING, for example. Some
fringe benefits are more psychological than material, such as the addition of a name-plate to a
manager's door when he or she reaches a certain
level in the corporate hierarchy.

Fringe benefits have the effect of disguising the
real VALUE of an employee's remuneration. For
many managers they can amount to over 30% of
salary, and they tend to tie employees more tight-
ly to one company by creating a mini-welfare
state, as it were, within the corporation.

FRN

See FLOATING-RATE NOTE.

FUTURES

Certain contracts in sophisticated commodity and
financial markets that oblige parties to the CON-
TRACT to do something in the future. These contracts are "tradeable", that is they can be bought
and sold on a "futures exchange". The most successful futures exchanges (which have been
growing rapidly in recent years) are in Chicago,
New York, London, Paris and Singapore.

Futures allow companies and investors to
"hedge" their positions, that is to reduce the risk
from future price movements. Suppose a COM-
PANY has a FORWARD CONTRACT to supply 40
tonnes of orange juice in six months' time at a
price of, say, $x. It can immediately buy a futures
contract in Chicago that will ensure the delivery
of that 40 tonnes of orange juice in exactly six
months' time. If such a contract costs the company $y, it will know there and then what PROFIT it
is to make on the orange-juice deal: $(x-y) before
transport costs.

G

GASTARBEITER
German for "guest worker", a migrant worker
from a poor country invited to do unskilled
LABOUR in a rich country. *Gastarbeiter* are expected to return to their homeland after a period.
They do not, therefore, have the same rights (or
incur the same costs) as local employees.

GATT
See GENERAL AGREEMENT ON TARIFFS AND TRADE.

GEARING
The ratio between a COMPANY's debt and its EQUI-
TY, known in the USA as leverage. In the 1980s,
when banks were keen to lend to corporations,
the ratio was held to be a key indicator of a company's borrowing capacity. It was always flawed
as an indicator, however. What good was equity
when a recession came, when interest rates rose,
and the company could no longer repay its debts
on time?

More helpful was something called "income
gearing", the proportion of a company's PROFIT
being used to pay interest (on its loans).

GENERAL AGREEMENT ON TARIFFS AND TRADE
An international agreement signed by 22 countries when it was first drawn up in 1947, but since
signed by over 100 countries, accounting for
around 90% of all the world's merchandise trade.

In its own words, the aim of the General
Agreement on Tariffs and Trade (GATT) is:

*To provide a secure and predictable international
trading environment for the business community,
and a continuing process of trade liberalisation
in which investment, job creation and trade can
thrive. In this way, the multilateral trading system
contributes to economic growth and development
throughout the world.*

The GATT attempts to persuade countries to get
rid of quotas, and it acts as the secretariat for a
series of multinational discussions (called "Rounds")

which aim to reduce tariffs.

The latest is called the Uruguay Round, and it is attempting to tackle areas of trade that have traditionally been excluded from the GATT's remit, such as agriculture, services and INTELLECTUAL PROPERTY.

The GATT's main problem is that it has few teeth. When it is notified of PROTECTIONISM there is little it can do but rely on the argument that the consequences of retaliation by others will be worse than the consequences of allowing free trade.

GO-SLOW

An industrial practice that is something less than a STRIKE, but more than a WORK-TO-RULE. Workers take every opportunity to slow down the production process, or the rate at which they provide a service, in order to bring pressure on their employer during a wage negotiation. In some companies the difference between a go-slow and normal service is not immediately apparent.

GOING PRIVATE

The transformation of a PUBLIC COMPANY into a private company, the opposite of "GOING PUBLIC". It is the ambition of most businesses to go public. Nevertheless, in the UK in recent years two famous companies, having chosen to go public, have subsequently changed their minds and reverted to being private: Richard Branson's Virgin group, and Andrew Lloyd Webber's Really Useful Company, owner of the rights to Lloyd Webber musicals such as *Cats*.

GOING PUBLIC

The process of transforming a private COMPANY owned by a few shareholders into a PUBLIC COMPANY whose shares can be traded among members of the public, and whose share price is quoted on a stock exchange. Going public can be expensive, requiring the services of an investment bank (to prepare the documentation), plus considerable legal and accounting fees.

G

In Anglo-Saxon economies going public is the pot of gold at the end of the rainbow for most entrepreneurs. It enables them to sell some of their shares, and thereby to cash in on their creation.

GOLDEN HANDCUFFS
A form of reward given to key employees that ties them to the COMPANY and/or (perhaps just as importantly) prevents them from working for a rival. Golden handcuffs come in several shapes, each with its own degree of gilt. For example:

* a cheap long-term loan which the employer knows the employee will have difficulty in paying back at short notice;
* a lump sum payment in return for a contractual obligation not to work for a rival for a stated period of time.

Golden handcuffs extend more widely than is generally appreciated. Any employee with a pension or a company car is handcuffed by the inconvenience (and expense) of buying a new car and/or changing pension schemes.

GOLDEN PARACHUTE
An expression coined in the 1980s to describe the employment contracts that top managers (mostly in the USA) wrote for themselves when they felt that their COMPANY might be subject to a TAKEOVER, and that they might be out of a job. The contracts stipulated that should such a situation occur, the managers would receive huge compensation on their dismissal. In some cases the compensation was to be paid even if the managers were merely pushed to one side, and not actually dismissed.

Such abuses of MANAGEMENT's power should, of course, be checked by shareholders. But they often see golden parachutes as a deterrent to takeovers which they themselves may not relish.

GOODWILL
The amount that an acquiring COMPANY (A) pays

for another company (B) over and above the VALUE of B's ASSETS. Goodwill is thus the amount paid for the fact that there is more to B than meets an accountant's eye. It includes:

- the goodwill (in the literal sense) of its customers;
- the value of its brands;
- the value of its unfinished research and development, and
- the value of its MANAGEMENT team.

None of these appear in the annual ACCOUNTS. After an ACQUISITION this intangible "goodwill" has to be dealt with in the accounts of the merged company.

In the USA it is usually deducted from profits gradually over a number of years. In the UK it is more often deducted immediately from company RESERVES.

GREENFIELD SITE

A site for a new FACTORY or office that has hitherto been unused for industrial or commercial purposes. Such sites are situated on what were previously green fields; for example, in small industrial estates on the fringes of old towns, or in new industrial towns such as Milton Keynes or Sophie Antipolis.

Greenfield sites sound pretty, but they are often soulless. Where do you go for lunch, or for a change of scene? The Japanese favour them, however, for their new operations abroad. They prefer to start with a clean industrial slate rather than a long-standing business set in its ways.

GUARANTEE

There are four main commercial meanings.

1 A promise given by a manufacturer that an article sold is of a certain quality. If the article is found to be faulty within a specified period, the manufacturer guarantees to mend or replace it.

2 A promise by a third party to pay a debt should certain conditions not be fulfilled by the parties to the debt CONTRACT. This is helpful, for example, when new companies are trying to raise a loan; the directors give personal guarantees. If the COMPANY does not repay the loan, then they do.

3 A bank guarantee is a written promise from a bank to repay a debt to a third party if the DEBTOR does not do so by a certain date.

4 A performance guarantee is an amount (normally 5–10% of the VALUE of a contract) that a customer withholds from a supplier until the contract is completely fulfilled.

HARD SELL

A MARKETING term to describe very aggressive ways of selling products or services. Certain industries are renowned for their hard-sell methods: time-sharing (of holiday homes); life insurance; and the business of Christmas, for example.

Hard sell is the opposite of soft sell, a marketing technique so subtle that its effect is almost subliminal. A soft sell involves the use of images and design to associate a product with a particular lifestyle or pleasurable situation (like falling in love).

HARDWARE

The pots and pans of the COMPUTER world; those bits of computer equipment that you can kick: the visual display unit (VDU); the keyboard; the DISK DRIVE; and the printer. The opposite of SOFTWARE.

Hard work never killed anybody. But worrying about it did.

Anon

HEAD OFFICE

For top managers, a clubhouse; for the rest, an excuse for inaction as in: "I'll have to ask head office".

One of industry's most significant discoveries in the 1980s was that it did not need the huge head offices favoured in the 1960s and 1970s. These grandiose buildings contained two types of worker, both of whom became increasingly redundant.

• **The corporate planners.** These people could spend weeks transcribing the minutiae of a COMPANY's future plans. As the pace of change increased, the need for this precision diminished. Long-term plans were out-of-date the day after they were written.
• **The information pushers.** These people

channelled information from the top of the corporation downwards and outwards. Less frequently they pushed it in the opposite direction. Computers and INFORMATION TECHNOLOGY took over their function far more efficiently.

HEAVY INDUSTRY

Any manufacturer who makes big things (like ships) with big machines and weighty RAW MATERIALS. "Heavy" sounds serious, as opposed to its opposite – "light industry" – which sounds frivolous; but it is light industry that keeps the western world wealthy. Heavy industry is increasingly being dispersed to developing countries.

HIGH-TECH

Something that is technologically advanced: "The COMPANY is moving into high-tech businesses like body scanners and colour photocopiers". There is an impression that high-tech is good; and low-tech bad. Yet some of the most profitable businesses are in low-tech industries.

As with HEAVY INDUSTRY, high-tech demonstrates how the choice of language in business influences the way we think of business. High-tech sounds modern; low-tech sounds base. The reality is very different.

HISTORIC COST

The starting point for almost all accounting calculations: the COST of a COMPANY'S ASSET when it was originally purchased. Accountants like this because it is a real amount of money that was once actually paid by somebody, unlike some other costs which are mere theoretical calculations.

The trouble with historic cost is that it takes no note of the passage of time. DEPRECIATION is the technique that accountants use to take account of the effects of wear and tear on a company's assets, and of the fact that companies need to put aside money to replace an asset as and when it is worn out. The cost of replacing an asset that was bought five years ago may be more or less than it was then. It will certainly not be the same.

HUMAN-RESOURCE MANAGEMENT

The now common expression for all aspects of management dealing with people. It is wider than the old-fashioned expression "personnel management". Whereas personnel management is involved only with the nitty-gritty of employees' lives – their pensions, company cars, health check-ups, and so on – human-resource management covers wider policy issues like TRAINING, recruitment and RELOCATION.

IMF
See INTERNATIONAL MONETARY FUND.

IMPORT QUOTA
A form of PROTECTIONISM in which a country sets a limit (a quota) on the quantity (or weight) of certain goods that it will allow to be imported across its borders. Import quotas can be very precisely targeted at a specific exporting country, product or time, and are thus a useful riposte in a trade war. They can often be circumvented, however, by passing the goods through a third country.

INCENTIVE
Anything that encourages an employee to work harder and to be more productive. An "incentive bonus" is a bonus paid for production that is in excess of an agreed amount; a variation on the PIECE-RATE system.

INCOME STATEMENT
See PROFIT AND LOSS ACCOUNT.

INDIRECT COST
A COST that cannot be directly attributed to a particular product. Such costs include the wages of employees who work on the manufacture of several products (general managers or supervisors, for example), and the cost of machines that are used in the manufacture of more than one product.

These costs have to be allocated to each product in one way or another in order to calculate the price at which the product is to be sold profitably.

If you've nothing nice to say about anybody, pull up a chair.
Anon

INDUSTRIAL ACTION
See STRIKE.

INDUSTRIAL ESPIONAGE

Spying on companies to obtain secrets for somebody else's commercial benefit. In most countries the law is remarkably unclear about whether it is illegal to steal trade secrets or not. In one case an industrial spy was jailed for stealing paper from his employer, not for stealing the sensitive company information that was on the paper.

When secrets disappear across a border it is even more difficult to obtain legal redress. The absence of adequate patents and recognition of INTELLECTUAL PROPERTY rights in many countries means that the international theft of ideas is big business, particularly in the pharmaceutical and COMPUTER industries. There have been several major cases involving the theft by Japanese companies of computer-industry secrets from US firms.

During the cold war East Germany was reckoned to have had more industrial spies in West Germany than political ones. Their intelligence saved East Germany billions of dollars a year. In the post-cold war era East-West political espionage may fade away, but its industrial espionage will not.

INDUSTRIAL PSYCHOLOGY

The study of human behaviour in a working environment. This is a favourite area of study for MANAGEMENT academics whose work has focused on a number of areas.

- **Team building.** How to make groups work better together, a skill the Japanese have developed to a high degree.
- **MOTIVATION.** What makes workers more productive: the fact that "soft" factors (like feeling needed) are as important as hard factors like pay and FRINGE BENEFITS.
- **LEADERSHIP.** What does it take to be a COMPANY boss? Can the skills be learnt? Can potential leaders be identified at an early stage?

INDUSTRIAL RELATIONS

A subject that has a more narrow meaning than

its name implies. It does not cover the whole range of relations in industry – between supplier and manufacturer, manufacturer and customer, and so on – but only the narrow subject of relations between employers, trade unions and the government departments that watch over them.

Industrial relations are like sexual relations, better when done between consenting parties.
Vic Feather, when general secretary of the UK's TUC

INDUSTRIAL REVOLUTION
Aptly called the "Industrial Revelation" in *1066 and All That*. The process of social and economic change whereby an agricultural country turns into a manufacturing one: farmers head for the cities and jobs in newly-opened factories.

The first industrial revolution occurred in the UK at the end of the eighteenth and beginning of the nineteenth centuries. Behind it were new ideas about MASS PRODUCTION and the division of LABOUR, and it was propelled by a spate of scientific inventions that came with the almost simultaneous discovery of steam and coal power.

INFLATION
The economic phenomenon of a general rise in prices. The most commonly used measure of inflation is the increase in the price of a "basket" of retail goods over a period of time. Very rarely in history have nations experienced a negative rate of inflation (that is an across-the-board fall in prices).

Some degree of inflation is generally accepted as inevitable. A very high rate is undesirable because of the uncertainty it creates, and because it hurts creditors (to the benefit of debtors) and those on fixed incomes.

One of the main causes of inflation is high growth in an economy's money supply; that is, sending out more notes and coins to chase a fixed amount of goods. The result is that the price of those goods rises.

*When I first started working I used to dream of
the day I might be earning the salary I'm now
starving on.*
Saying to show evils of inflation

INFORMATION TECHNOLOGY

The combination of computers and telecommunications, and the remarkable things that they
can achieve together. It is sometimes known
as informatics, more commonly as the simple
abbreviation, IT.

IT has changed the way in which companies
organise themselves. By making information
instantly available to almost anybody anywhere, it
has reduced the need for the type of middle manager who pushed paper from the top of the
organisation down to the bottom.

In turn, lower levels of employees now receive
more information, demanding a higher degree of
skill and judgment on their part. Information
technology has also encouraged companies to go
into new geographical markets, secure in the
knowledge that with IT they can keep a proper
eye on the business.

*Nothing is worse for morale than a lack of
information down in the ranks. I call it NETMA –
nobody ever tells me anything – and I have tried
to minimise that problem.*
Ed Carlson, when president of United Airlines

INNOVATION

A critical part of the business process: the addition of new elements to products or services, or
to the methods of producing them. Innovation is
not the creation of an entirely new product; that
is invention, and relatively rare. It is, rather, the
continuous process of adding to and improving a
product in order to gain an edge over its competitors. This can only be done by listening closely to
customers. Almost all IBM's early innovations

came from collaboration with its leading customer, the US Census Office.

Lowell Steele, for many years the manager responsible for innovation at General Electric, wrote an article for the *Harvard Business Review* in 1983 in which he listed seven popular misconceptions about technology.

1 The best technology possible should always be implemented.
2 What is "good enough" is always determined rationally.
3 Most innovations are successful.
4 MURPHY'S LAW does not apply to technical innovation.
5 The more original the idea, the better.
6 Technical success is the major hurdle that an innovation has to cross.
7 Routines, standards and similar constraints are not important in technology development.

Remember that Steele maintained that all seven of the above were wrong.

Innovation is 1% inspiration and 99% perspiration.
Thomas Edison

INSOLVENCY
The condition of a COMPANY that is unable to repay its debts as and when they become due. Insolvency is not necessarily fatal. Companies can attempt to reschedule their debts, either informally with their creditors, or formally through legal processes like ADMINISTRATION and CHAPTER 11.

INTANGIBLE ASSETS
ASSETS that cannot be kicked. An accounting term used to refer to things like GOODWILL, patents, brand names and trademarks, which have a VALUE even though they are (literally) intangible. While nobody denies that these things are worth some-

thing, problems arise when they try to decide how much.

INTELLECTUAL PROPERTY

Ideas, inventions, designs or books that belong to their creator. Although intellectual property can be protected by patent, registered TRADEMARK and COPYRIGHT, it is particularly vulnerable to theft. Western books and music are shamelessly copied in the Far East without the permission of the author or songwriter.

Intellectual property is set to be the next most contentious area of international trade. The International Trade Commission estimates that US companies alone lose $40 billion–50 billion a year (almost half the nation's trade deficit) from the unauthorised use of American technology by foreign manufacturers.

In a landmark judgment in a New Jersey court in 1992, the US computer company Honeywell was awarded $96m compensation for technology stolen by the Japanese camera company Minolta. From 1984 Honeywell inventions had been used by Minolta in its autofocus and automatic lens shutter cameras, and not a yen was paid to Honeywell in royalties.

As a result of its experience Honeywell believes that certain international rules are needed to protect intellectual property.

• Common standards for patents, trademarks and copyrights.
• A compatible international patent system.
• Mechanisms for a timely resolution of disputes (most logically within the GATT).
• Rigorous enforcement rules, including border controls.

INTEREST COVER

The number of times that a business can pay its interest out of its pre-tax profits. (Banks watch this figure keenly.) Likewise, DIVIDEND cover is the number of times that a COMPANY's dividends can be paid out of its pre-tax profits.

I

INTERFACE
The HARDWARE and SOFTWARE that lie between two computers, allowing them to communicate with each other. From this rather specialist technical meaning the word has come to be used (pretentiously) in many business contexts: "He had great difficulty interfacing with his colleagues from New York", or "The design process sits at the interface between production and consumption."

INTERIM MANAGER
See TROUBLESHOOTER.

The best investments are often those that looked dead wrong when they were made.

Anon

INTERNAL RATE OF RETURN
The internal rate of return (IRR) is the interest rate at which the discounted future CASH FLOW from a project exactly equals the investment in the project. In general, this must be higher than the marginal cost of CAPITAL for it to be worth going ahead with the project.

INTERNATIONAL MONETARY FUND
The International Monetary Fund (IMF) was set up to police the Bretton Woods Agreement, an international treaty signed in 1944 by all the world's major nations, pledging them to maintain fixed exchange rates between their currencies. The IMF has the power to lend considerable sums to member countries, based on the size of their "quota", that is, the membership subscriptions they pay which are roughly related to the size of their economies.

The IMF's principal function largely disappeared once fixed exchange rates were abandoned in the early 1970s. It found a new role for itself by becoming more involved with member countries' economic policies, and in particular with those of heavily indebted countries (for example, Brazil and Mexico) caught up in the international debt crisis of the early 1980s. With the break-up of Comecon in Eastern Europe, the IMF has found itself another significant role in overseeing the economic transformation from communism to capitalism of countries in the region.

INTERVIEW
It is important to structure interviews for jobs in a way that will get the best out of the candidates and also ensure that you get the best person for the job.

Here are the sort of questions that should feature in an interview.

- ❏ **Open questions.** To encourage the interviewee to talk, for example: "Why does this position interest you?"
- ❏ **Closed questions.** Requiring a yes or no answer: "Do you always meet your deadlines?"
- ❏ **Specific questions.** Asking for specific information, such as: "Which computer systems have you used?"
- ❏ **Reflective questions.** Looking back on remarks already made in the interview and connecting them to an area you are currently discussing, for instance: "You mentioned earlier ..." or "Can you explain ..."
- ❏ **Hypothetical questions.** To show the candidate's speed of thought and creativity, for example: "If you hadn't taken your last job, what do you think you might be doing now?"

INVENTORY
What the British call STOCK-IN-TRADE. The word inventory avoids confusion between stocks (the usual abbreviation for stock-in-trade) and stocks (as in stocks and shares).

IRR
See INTERNAL RATE OF RETURN.

IT
See INFORMATION TECHNOLOGY.

JIT
See JUST-IN-TIME.

JOB SHARING
A once fashionable way of dividing one full-time job between more than one part-time employee. In practice there are difficulties with job sharing, not the least being the fact that governments rarely treat two part-timers the same as one full-timer in terms of social security payments, and so on. Also there are many jobs that do not lend themselves to being handed over to somebody else at lunch-time.

Job sharing has proved reasonably successful in two specific situations.

• For women who do not want to work full-time because of other commitments. It suits those jobs that depend on serving a "client list" (home nursing, for example), such that the list can be easily divided.
• To soften the blow of REDUNDANCY on the production line; allowing two people to do a job part-time instead of randomly laying one of them off.

JOBBING
A system of production used when the quantity of goods to be produced is too small to justify either BATCH production or MASS PRODUCTION. Jobbing is often found in the engineering industry where orders (for machine tools, for instance) are in very small numbers. Such production needs particularly careful planning, each product requiring slightly different operations in a different sequence. With jobbing it is very difficult to forecast production times.

JOINT VENTURE
A business venture entered into jointly by two or more partners. Companies favour joint ventures when they are exploring a new MARKET or a new geographical region. Their main aim is to share the risk, but it helps if one of the partners has

some local or specialised knowledge of the market to be explored. Joint ventures have become popular as more companies have looked to new markets abroad.

Many joint ventures split up after a while, with the partners deciding to go their own separate ways. Although these splits are often acrimonious, they do not mean that the joint venture was a failure. It may just be a natural stage in this way of starting a business.

Some joint ventures have a long and impressive track record: Unilever, the Anglo-Dutch giant, is the result of a joint venture between the UK's Lever Brothers and the Netherlands' J. Van den Bergh. It is now far bigger than either of its founders.

JUST-IN-TIME
A technique of stock CONTROL that aims to minimise the amount of stocks that a manufacturing COMPANY has to hold. Developed in the 1960s by the Toyota car company in Japan, just-in-time (JIT) has come to assume magical powers as one of the techniques that contributed most to the Japanese industrial miracle.

The core of the idea is quite simple housekeeping: each stage in the production process calls for parts as and when it needs them. This can result in one unit receiving as many as ten deliveries a day. The system also breaks down the ASSEMBLY LINE operation into small units, each of which is responsible for delivery to another similarly small unit.

JIT probably works particularly well in Japan because it suits the Japanese mentality. Too much western individualism might literally throw a spanner in the works.

K

KICKBACK

In the USA, an illegal payment made in specific
circumstances; in particular, by an employee to
an employer who has agreed (with unions or
government) to pay a certain minimum wage. In
order to get the job at all, the employee agrees to
pay a percentage of his or her salary back to the
employer.

A kickback can also be a payment to a government official from a supplier for his or her help in
obtaining a particular PUBLIC-SECTOR contract.
Since such contracts are often huge, the temptation for both the briber and the bribed can be
very strong. (See PUBLIC PROCUREMENT.)

KNOW-HOW

A saleable technique or skill that has been developed by a COMPANY. For example, when JIT
was first developed it was known as the Toyota
manufacturing system. For a while, until other
companies adopted the idea, JIT was a part of
Toyota's know-how.

Know-how may be more tangibly attributed to
products: the recipe for Sara Lee's Pecan Pie, for
example, or the technique of semi-freezing prepared foods developed by Marks & Spencer.
Once it is widely available and widely used, however, its VALUE diminishes. When everybody
knows how, there is no know-how.

Facts are power.
Harold Geneen, CEO, ITT

KNOWLEDGE WORKER

A neologism for workers whose job depends on
their having access to knowledge about the corporation, knowledge that is disseminated by
INFORMATION TECHNOLOGY. Typically, knowledge
workers include airline sales staff or car-rental
staff: people who cannot do their job (selling tick-
ets or allocating cars) without computers to
inform them of what is available.

K

Knowledge workers are contrasted with old-style manual workers who learnt a skill and then repeated it again and again without any change in their work environment or any requirement for further information. Knowledge workers are constantly "interfacing" with their employer.

LABOUR

Human work, and one of the economists' three so-called "factors of production": land, labour and CAPITAL (see also FACTORY). Economists call the price of labour "wages".

The price of a manager, of course, is a salary and a bunch of perks (see FRINGE BENEFITS). Managers do not like to think that what they do is labour, but they use the word in a number of contexts.

- **Casual labour.** Workers, particularly in the construction industry, who work on and off, as and when needed.
- **Labour-intensive.** The sort of product or service that requires a high input of labour for every unit produced, and is therefore appropriately produced in a country with ample spare labour (see CAPITAL-INTENSIVE).
- **Labour mobility.** The willingness of workers to move from one home to another in order to start a new job.
- **Labour relations** (see INDUSTRIAL RELATIONS).

LAN

See LOCAL AREA NETWORK.

LAPTOP

A type of COMPUTER that can be used on the lap; particularly useful for business journeys by train and by plane, when there is a lot of spare time but not a lot of spare room.

A laptop computer is scarcely distinguishable from a "portable computer". The main difference is that some portable computers need to be plugged into a mains source of electricity. The essential feature of the laptop is that it can be run for a reasonable length of time on rechargeable batteries. The smallest laptops are often called notebook computers.

LAST IN, FIRST OUT

Commonly known by its acronym LIFO, it is the opposite of FIFO (FIRST IN, FIRST OUT). A method of accounting for stocks which assumes that the last stocks to be purchased are the first to be used in production.

The later the stocks are bought the more expensive they are. So LIFO effectively increases a COMPANY's costs. Hence under LIFO companies have lower profits than under FIFO. UK companies favour FIFO; continental European companies favour LIFO.

LEAD TIME
The time between placing an order for something and the receipt of it. Lead times are an important variable in the planning of production processes.

Any survey of what businessmen are reading runs smack into the open secret that most businessmen aren't.
Marilyn Bender

LEADERSHIP
An indefinable quality that makes some people good at activating others in a particular direction. That direction is not always benign: Attila the Hun, Napoleon and Hitler were all great leaders. So, arguably, were Al Capone and Robert Maxwell.

Companies and business schools spend an enormous amount of time trying to distil the essence of leadership. Here is one attempt from Abraham Zaleznik, a respected academic in the field, who believes that natural leaders have the following characteristics.

• They are active rather than reactive, shaping ideas rather than responding to them.
• They take a personal and active attitude towards goals and ambitions.
• They develop quite fresh ways of looking at old problems.
• They are more interested in what events mean to others than in their own role in getting

things accomplished.
• They are often viewed with strong emotion by others.
• They tend to feel somewhat apart from their environment and from other people.

LEASING

The hiring of expensive ASSETS, like machinery, by a manufacturer from a financial COMPANY. This is obviously useful for manufacturers who cannot afford to pay the full COST of the assets. It is also (less obviously) a clever scheme to benefit fully from tax allowances. Manufacturers often pay too little tax to enable them to take advantage of all the allowances on their purchase of capital goods. Finance companies pay plenty of tax against which to set capital allowances. Put the two together, share the allowances, and you have leasing.

"Lease-back" refers to the practice whereby a company sells a building that it owns to a property or finance company and immediately leases it back. This releases cash that the company can use for other purposes.

LETTER OF CREDIT

An arrangement with a bank to obtain payment, usually abroad. A bank writes a letter to another bank in which it gives the right to a third party to draw money up to a stated amount, an amount for which the writer of the letter takes responsibility.

It sounds complicated but it is not. The first bank is usually writing the letter on behalf of a customer (whose account is debited with the amount in question). This customer is buying something from the customer of the second bank who wants to be sure of getting the money before the goods are shipped.

There are a number of different types of letter of credit (L/C).

• Confirmed L/C. This carries a promise from the vendor's bank that it will be responsible for any credit given to its customer.

- Documentary L/C. This is an L/C to which the vendor has to attach a number of documents (such as a BILL OF LADING or a consular seal) before being paid.
- Irrevocable L/C. This is an L/C that cannot be revoked without the permission of the person to whom the payment is being made.

LETTER OF INTENT
A written declaration that the writer intends to follow a particular course of action (such as buying another COMPANY) if certain things happen; for example, if the company's books are as they say they are when the writer examines them. A letter of intent is not a legally binding promise. It is little better than the word of the person who writes it.

LEVERAGE
See GEARING.

LIABILITIES
Things on the opposite side of a BALANCE SHEET to ASSETS: what is owed by a business to its creditors. A COMPANY's assets minus its liabilities equal its NET WORTH, the underlying VALUE belonging to its shareholders.

LICENSING
The granting to somebody of a right which it would otherwise be illegal for them to exercise. For example, a pharmaceutical COMPANY may give somebody a licence to sell in a foreign MARKET a drug which is still protected by patent.

LIFO
See LAST IN, FIRST OUT.

LIMITED LIABILITY
One of the great inventions of capitalism: the granting to a COMPANY by law of a limit to its liability. For a company limited by shares the maximum liability is the share capital, effectively the

amount still unpaid on the shares (see CAPITAL); for a company limited by guarantee the maximum liability is the amount that the members of the company have guaranteed to pay in the event of LIQUIDATION.

For companies to retain this privilege they have to follow certain rules. They and their owners have to be registered with the relevant authorities, and they have to indicate clearly in their literature that they are "limited" in this way.

The consequence of limited liability is that every business has to live with the reality of bad and DOUBTFUL DEBTS, the result of doing business with limited companies that have overreached their limit. Without limited liability, however, every DIRECTOR or owner of a company could be personally liable for all of the company's debts. In that case scarcely anybody would ever be prepared to start a new business, and we would still live in a world of small craftsmen and medieval guilds.

LINE MANAGEMENT

Those managers who are primarily responsible for the actual production of a COMPANY's goods and services. This classification is an analogy with the military, where line duties are those in the front line of fighting, while staff duties are those in support.

In companies, too, staff managers provide support services for the line managers, such as planning, personnel, shipping, and so on. Many find the distinction between line and staff jobs increasingly artificial. There are few line jobs that have no involvement with, say, planning or personnel.

LIQUID ASSETS

Any ASSETS that can be quickly turned into cash without loss; for example, bank deposits or government SECURITIES. Many more assets can, of course, be sold quickly, but they are not liquid if the seller would have to sell them at a loss in order to sell them quickly.

LIQUIDATION

The corporate equivalent of execution and burial. The tidying up of a COMPANY's affairs when it ceases to do business. This is usually because the company is unable to pay its debts, but it may occur because the company's owners have decided that it has achieved what it set out to do (referred to as a voluntary WINDING-UP).

The corporate undertaker (called the liquidator) is usually an accountant or a solicitor, but does not have to be. His or her main job is to ascertain the exact amount owed to the company's creditors, and then to sell the company's ASSETS in order to pay back the creditors as much as possible.

However, not all creditors are equal. Some have priority over others. Secured creditors are paid first, followed by preferential creditors like the liquidator and the tax collector. The rest follow, *pari passu.*

LIQUIDITY

The amount of short-term ASSETS held by a business, and its ability to turn them into cash at short notice. A COMPANY's liquidity is said to be high if these assets form a large percentage of its total assets. Liquidity is important to companies in helping them ride over temporary aberrations in their markets, or over a sudden cash crisis.

Net liquidity is a company's short-term assets minus its short-term LIABILITIES. Various ratios are used to test a company's level of liquidity.

• The current ratio: of current assets to current liabilities.
• The ACID TEST: of cash and easily realisable assets to current liabilities.
• The average time it takes to collect trade debts.

Bank of America developed a list of nine warning signals which indicate to it that a company is getting into trouble. They are listed from the most to the least common.

- ❑ Delays in submitting financial statements.
- ❑ A decline in bank deposits and an increasing incidence of returned cheques.
- ❑ A failure to perform on other obligations (for example, slow repayment of the personal debt of individual directors).
- ❑ An INVENTORY glut.
- ❑ An increase in delinquent payments with more and more straying past their due date.
- ❑ Difficulty in arranging meetings or visits.
- ❑ Legal action against the business.
- ❑ Increasing debtors.
- ❑ Negative information about the business from its competitors and customers.

LOCAL AREA NETWORK
A local area NETWORK (LAN) is a COMPUTER network covering a small geographical area; for example, a government department.

LOCK-OUT
The exclusion, from a FACTORY or office, of one group of employees by another group. Lock-outs usually occur when there are disputes between MANAGEMENT and TRADE UNIONS. Sometimes they are intertwined with a STRIKE. Managers may lock out blue-collar workers who decide unilaterally to return to work after a strike.

LOSS LEADER
A product that is sold below COST in order to entice consumers into buying other products. Loss leaders are a MARKETING device promoted by retailers. A number of manufacturers object to their products being sold as loss leaders.

M

MACHINE TOOL
A piece of equipment used for cutting or shaping metal. Machine tools range from simple drills and lathes to the sophisticated pieces of equipment required to prepare metal for use in aircraft, cars or satellites.

MACHINE LOADING
The allocation of specific tasks to individual machines within a FACTORY; the responsibility of the production control manager.

MAINTENANCE
The COST of keeping plant and equipment running efficiently. This is generally only the actual cost incurred in servicing the equipment. It does not include the OPPORTUNITY COST of having equipment out of operation while it is being serviced.

MAN-BY-THE-WINDOW
The unsuccessful Japanese manager is given a daily newspaper, no responsibilities and a desk by the window. The German equivalent is slightly different: he is the "*weit weg vom Fenster*", the man far away from the window.

The worst part about success is trying to find someone who is happy for you.
Old saying

MANAGEMENT
Either the group of managers who together run a business; or the art of so doing. The word "manage" is several centuries old and it comes from the Italian *manneggiare* "to handle" (horses).

It is widely acknowledged that effective management requires a number of particular abilities.

- To listen as well as to talk.
- To lead by example.
- To give clear instructions when required.

- To select able people.
- To know how to encourage people to be innovative.
- To give credit when credit is due.
- To be honest, consistent, approachable and decisive.
- To be able to delegate.

Management is an activity or art where those who have not yet succeeded and those who have proved unsuccessful are led by those who have not yet failed.
Paulsson Frenckner

Men are made to be managed and women are born managers.
George Meredith

To manage is to forecast and to plan, to organise, to command, to co-ordinate and to control.
Henri Fayol

MANAGEMENT ACCOUNTS
An occasion for accountants to break free from the rules and regulations that permeate other areas of their work (such as auditing). Management accounts are prepared as a tool to aid managers in the CONTROL and forward planning of their business. They can be selective in what they measure and subjective in the ways that they measure it. To be really useful they must be:

- simple and easy to read;
- frequent and consistent; and
- produced promptly after the period that they are measuring.

MANAGEMENT BUY-IN/BUY-OUT
A popular phenomenon in the 1980s. Teams of managers borrowed large sums of money from banks in order to buy companies which they then ran and the banks used the company's ASSETS as

collateral for the loans.

In a management buy-out (MBO), the team of managers comes from inside the company and buys out the existing owners; in a management buy-in (the less common of the two), a team of managers from outside the company buys into it.

Since most deals are highly leveraged (see GEARING), the managers are handicapped from the start by having to service a high level of debt. Many MBOs fell apart when interest rates rose in the 1990s.

MANAGEMENT BY OBJECTIVES

A popular phrase used to describe MANAGEMENT systems where employees agree jointly with senior managers as to what are to be their objectives (or ultimate goals) in the job. They then track their progress in moving towards those goals with the managers.

MANAGEMENT DEVELOPMENT

A catch-all phrase referring to the teaching and nurturing of management skills (for example, team-building or negotiation) rather than the teaching of specific technical skills (like engineering or accounting).

Any systematic training of managers depends on having a clear knowledge of what managers need to do. There are eight functions that are generally agreed to be central to the job of managing.

- Planning
- Organising
- Staffing
- Supervising
- Directing
- Controlling
- Co-ordinating
- Innovating

MARGIN

In general an amount of money "at the edge". In economic theory the margin is that level of production at which the COST of producing one more item is equal to the revenue to be gained from it. Marginal cost is the extra cost of producing one more unit of an article over and above an agreed output.

• **Profit margin.** The difference between the cost of something and the amount for which it is sold (see MARK-UP). All businesses need to know the full cost of their goods and services in order to know at what selling price they will have an acceptable profit margin.

• **Margin lending.** Lending by banks backed by the VALUE of shares. Banks will usually lend up to a certain percentage (about 60%) of the value of shares. If the shares' value declines, the bank will ask the borrower to repay an amount so that the loan remains at 60% of the (lower) value of the shares backing it. This type of lending has got many wealthy people into trouble.

• **Margin trading.** The buying of SECURITIES through a BROKER while only putting up part of the cost of the securities, the rest coming as a loan from the broker. In effect this is the eternally dangerous practice of gambling with borrowed money.

MARK-UP
The profit MARGIN related to COST. If a retailer sells something for $125 which costs $100, the profit margin is $25, or 20% (one-fifth) of the selling price. The retailer's mark-up is also $25, but it is 25% (one-quarter) of the cost price.

MARKET
The place where buyers (that is, demand) and sellers (that is, supply) come together to trade in goods and services and to determine their prices. Such a place can be as large as a country, "sales in the US market were weak last year", or as small as a single building, "traders on the London STOCKMARKET keep bumping into each other". "Market economics" refers to the setting of prices in an economy by markets rather than by

regulators or governments.

"Market" can also be the total VALUE of all sales in a market place. Hence "market share" refers to the percentage share of those sales belonging to a product or business; for example, "BMW has an 8% share of the car market in Japan." The market leader is that product or COMPANY with the largest market share.

A stable competitive market never has more than three significant competitors, the largest of which has no more than four times the market share of the smallest.
Boston Consulting Group's "Rule of Three and Four"

MARKETING
According to the Institute of Marketing this is "the management process of identifying, anticipating and satisfying customer requirements profitably". Another definition is "the process of taking the guesswork out of hunch".

Marketing includes functions like ADVERTISING, MARKET RESEARCH, PRICING, sales promotion and testing new products ("test marketing"). In large companies all these responsibilites often come under a single "marketing" department. In smaller businesses they are either bought in from outside firms (advertising and market research, in particular), or they are the direct responsibility of someone not far from the chief executive.

Not everything that goes by the name of "marketing" deserves it. It has become too fashionable. A grave-digger remains a grave-digger even when called a mortician. Only the cost of burial goes up.
Peter Drucker

MARKET RESEARCH
The process of methodically investigating a

potential MARKET for a new product, or of examining the market for an existing product and the way it has changed (or might be about to change). Market research involves asking a sample of people a number of questions about a product, service or a COMPANY. This can be done in many ways: at random on the street, in structured discussion groups, by telephone, or by written questionnaire. The answers are then analysed statistically in order to examine the (potential) market along a number of different dimensions: age, geography, social status, and so on.

MASS PRODUCTION
The production of large quantities of standard items using ECONOMIES OF SCALE to keep the COST of each item as low as possible. (See also BATCH and JOBBING.)

> *The technology of mass production is inherently violent, ecologically damaging, self-defeating in terms of non-renewable resources, and stultifying for the human person.*
> E.F. Schumacher

MASTER'S DEGREE IN BUSINESS ADMINISTRATION
A post-graduate (and usually post-experience) general training in business and management. In the USA (where most universities now offer degrees in business administration) the Master's Degree in Business Administration (MBA) course usually lasts two years; in Europe it tends to be condensed into one year; in Japan it does not exist (or it takes a lifetime of work experience?).

Most MBA courses have a core of compulsory subjects plus a number of elective courses from which students can choose those that best suit them. The range of subjects varies, but it usually includes staples such as:

- accounting and finance;
- organisational behaviour;

- marketing;
- operations;
- human-resource management;
- economics and business policy.

The electives might include such things as international business, INFORMATION TECHNOLOGY, small businesses, or health-services management.

The number of students enrolling for MBA courses has increased rapidly in recent years. The USA now turns out more than 70,000 MBAs every year. At the same time the number of universities and colleges offering MBA courses has increased dramatically. This means that the most important thing to a potential employer is not whether a candidate has got an MBA (for they are two a penny), but where he or she got it from. An MBA is no longer of itself a passport to a world of six-figure salaries.

MATERIALS HANDLING

A key part of the production process, involving the movement of components and products around a FACTORY, or from one factory to another. The COST of materials handling can account for up to 40% of total manufacturing cost, and it is the cause of many industrial accidents. Efficient materials handling will try to ensure that:

- materials always move towards completion;
- they move as short a distance as possible;
- they are carried by similar devices; and
- they are carried with as little effort as possible.

MBA

See MASTER'S DEGREE IN BUSINESS ADMINISTRATION.

MBO

See MANAGEMENT BUY-IN/BUY-OUT.

MEAN

The average of a series of numbers. There are three different types of mean.

1 The arithmetic mean. The sum of all the numbers divided by the number of numbers; the most basic "average".

2 The geometric mean. This is calculated by multiplying all the numbers in the series together and then taking the nth root of that multiple, where n is the number of numbers. The geometric mean is useful where values change over time; it is always less than the arithmetic mean.

3 The weighted mean. This is a method of taking account of the fact that not all the numbers in the series will have the same significance. Thus before the mean is calculated, the more important numbers are "weighted". This involves multiplying them by a factor which reflects their importance.

MIDDLE MANAGER

An unflattering term referring to the large number of managers who are neither at the top of the managerial ladder nor obviously at the bottom of it.

Middle managers are often based at a COMPANY's head office, filling out the corporate pyramid between the directors and the line managers.

MANAGEMENT gurus have forecast a gloomy future for middle managers.

As long ago as 1954 Peter Drucker said that seven layers of management was the most that any company needed.

More recently, a report by the top management consultants McKinsey said:

The first step in accomplishing successful plant-floor implementation of new manufacturing approaches is the clearing out of all middle managers and support-service layers that clog the wheels of change.

MINIMUM WAGE

In some countries governments determine a wage which is the least that any full-time employee can legally be paid. The setting of such a wage encourages the growth of a black MARKET in LABOUR, where wages are below the legal minimum and where employees have no legal protection from exploitation.

TRADE UNIONS and MANAGEMENT also sometimes agree between themselves on minimum wages that are to be paid for particular jobs.

MINORITY INTEREST

When a COMPANY owns more than 50%, but less than 100%, of another company (its SUBSIDIARY), the other shareholders (who own less than 50%) are called "the minority interest".

A company's ACCOUNTS will embrace all its subsidiary company's ASSETS and LIABILITIES. There will be a separate item representing its obligation to the minority shareholders in its subsidiaries.

Minority interests have a degree of legal protection against exploitation by the majority.

MISSION STATEMENT

A statement by a COMPANY of its overriding business goals, of how it is going to achieve them, and of the values it will uphold in doing so. After a visit to Sears, Roebuck in the USA in the 1920s the founders of Marks & Spencer, then a rather ordinary general store, redefined their mission as:

The subversion of the class structure of nineteenth-century England by making available to the working and lower-middle classes, upper-class goods of better than upper-class quality at prices the working and lower-middle classes could well afford.

Few companies have such a precise (or socially ambitious) mission statement.

Much attention has recently been focused on the value of mission statements as a tool for creating team spirit and unity of purpose among a company's workforce by giving workers an idea of a higher purpose to their LABOUR.

To achieve their aim, mission statements must be:

- the result of some sort of consensus throughout the company of what it is about;
- clear and memorable;
- widely known and widely disseminated throughout the corporation;
- realistic, and not based on some far-flung ambition that employees cannot relate to.

MNC
See MULTINATIONAL COMPANY.

MODEM
A shortened form of modulator-demodulator, the instrument which is attached between a COMPUTER and a telephone line to allow computer messages to be converted into telephonic messages and sent around the world. Without the modem there would be no informatics (see INFORMATION TECHNOLOGY).

MONOPOLY
The total absence of COMPETITION: the situation where a single producer has the whole of a MARKET to itself. It is usually assumed that a COMPANY which has a monopoly will abuse its position by increasing prices way above what they would be if the company were in competition. The extra profits this makes are called monopoly profits.

> *How come there's only one Monopolies Commission?*
> Graffiti

Some monopolies have official approval; for example, those granted by patents on new drugs and inventions. These are granted for a limited period, however, and are a reward for the COST of the research that went into originally creating the product.

Monopolies are rarely "pure" in practice for two reasons.

- Very few (if any) products or services are so self-contained that they are not subject to some competition. The USA's regional newspapers and Europe's nationalised electricity industries are near-monopolies; but the newspapers compete with television and electricity competes with gas.
- Governments make an effort to ensure that those near-monopolies which do exist are not abused. Many nationalised industries have regulatory bodies to CONTROL their prices. Takeovers and acquisitions in sensitive sectors (such as newspapers) are closely monitored by anti-trust authorities.

The great achievement of Mr Sloan of General Motors was to structure this gigantic firm in such a manner that it became in fact a federation of fairly reasonably sized firms.
E.F. Schumacher

MOTIVATION

What moves people to behave in particular ways. Motivation is an important subject in several business areas. What motivates consumers to buy one thing and not another? What motivates employees to work hard? What motivates shareholders to be less than indifferent? Here are some useful tips.

❐ Remember that different people respond to different incentives and styles of management.
❐ Manage the overall problem-solving process; let staff manage the problems.
❐ Work with a team to identify their strengths and weaknesses and encourage them to develop their full potential.
❐ Involve the team in the early stages of projects.
❐ Do not keep all the interesting and creative work to yourself.
❐ Let your team help you.
❐ Give frequent and specific feedback: both positive and negative.

M

MULTINATIONAL COMPANY

A COMPANY which has production and MARKETING
operations in more than one country. Multinational companies (MNCs) are nothing new. In the early
years of this century US companies like Kellogg
and Singer had several production facilities outside the USA.

However, these early multinationals operated
like a series of independent national operations,
largely because communications and transport
systems were slow and inefficient. Each national
business was forced to plan and operate as an
independent unit. Only in recent years (with the
help of sophisticated air transport and telecommunications) have multinationals come to work
more as a single unit across the globe. People
have looked for a new word to describe this new
type of modern multinational: global company or
transnational, for example.

In fact, however, the very global Coca-Cola is
still dominated by its headquarters in Atlanta.

MULTINATIONAL ENTERPRISE

Another term for MULTINATIONAL COMPANY, often
abbreviated to MNE.

MURPHY'S LAW

The rule in business that if something can go
wrong then it will go wrong. Murphy is a common Irish surname, and an uncommon word for
potato.

NATIONALISATION

The taking over by government of privately-owned companies. Nationalisation is the opposite of PRIVATISATION, and a highly charged political issue. Socialist parties tend to favour nationalisation and conservative parties privatisation, though the issue is rarely cut and dried. France's socialist president, François Mitterrand, actually decreased the size of the state's shareholdings in French industry.

There are three occasions when the arguments in favour of nationalisation are strongest.

1 When a company has a near-MONOPOLY in its MARKET, and the state takes over in order to prevent the company from taking unfair advantage of its position.

2 When a company is in a sensitive area (such as defence) and it is in a nation's best interest that CONTROL of that company does not fall into "undesirable" hands.

3 In new industries that a country considers it is strategically important to be involved in, but which the private sector is unable (or unwilling) to nurture. In developed countries this is usually in new HIGH-TECH areas like semiconductors; in developing countries it is more often in heavy industries like steel, where the government does not want to be entirely dependent on imports.

If you want to make sure that crime doesn't pay, put it in the hands of the government.
Anon

NEGOTIATION

There are a million bits of advice (and at least as many advisers) on how to negotiate successfully. Here is one that has two advantages: it is short (four tips only); and it is associated with Harvard Business School (and known as the Harvard Negotiation Project Rules), so it should be good.

❑ Separate the people you are negotiating with from the problem; do not let emotions and personalities get in the way, but do let emotions show. This is contrary to the traditional "poker-face" approach to negotiation.

❑ Focus on interests not positions. It requires trust to expose your real underlying interest in negotiations, rather than some pose struck to create a particular impression.

❑ Search for new ideas that will be to both parties' benefit.

❑ Stick to objective criteria: from financial statements or market data.

NETWORK

A system that links a number of computers (via a central processing unit – CPU) so that they can share one DATABASE and gain access to each other's files. Like the word "INTERFACE", network has gained a wider currency from its computer usage. Networking, or making contacts, is what businessmen are supposed to be doing when they attend business cocktail parties and overseas conferences.

Networking also means a popular way for service firms (like lawyers and accountants) to build up an international presence without the CAPITAL COST of opening offices in dozens of cities. Linked together under some sort of loose umbrella organisation, firms in different countries agree to pool their resources as and when necessary. Loose structures of this sort, however, create problems of their own. Charging for the various little favours that are demanded becomes very difficult. Yet depending on strangers to return favours is unreliable. Inevitably, one partner in the network feels unfairly "put upon".

NET PRESENT VALUE

A mathematical concept used to measure the viability of an investment project. Net present value (NPV) is the difference between the present value of the future revenues of the project, and the present value of its future costs. The present value is calculated by discounting the future revenues and costs by the COST of CAPITAL.

NET WORTH

A COMPANY'S ASSETS less its LIABILITIES. "Tangible net worth" is the same equation, but with INTANGIBLE ASSETS (like GOODWILL) subtracted from the total. Net worth is that part of the company that would be left for its shareholders were all its assets to be sold for the amounts that the accountants claim they are worth. "Net asset backing" is the net worth per SHARE.

NICHE MARKET

A small sector of a MARKET. *The Economist*, for example, is in a niche publishing market: the market for international news magazines. Apple is in a niche market in the COMPUTER industry, unlike, say, IBM which aims to be all things to all computer users.

Small innovative businesses are particularly good at identifying niche markets, and then settling down cosily in them. Big companies frequently ignore them as being too small to be worth their while; but, as Apple has shown, a carefully identified niche can become a very big market indeed.

NIMBY

See NOT IN MY BACK YARD.

NPV

See NET PRESENT VALUE.

NON-TARIFF BARRIER

A barrier to trade that is not in the form of a TARIFF imposed on an import at its point of entry. Non-tariff barriers can take many forms. At their most crude they come in the form of quotas: ceilings on the quantity of goods or services that can be imported.

More subtly they take the form of a distribution system that discriminates in favour of locally produced goods – a non-tariff barrier that Japan is frequently accused of having – or of government regulation that (in banking, for example) only allows people to operate who are known to the local community.

Another popular non-tariff barrier comes in the form of standard safety requirements for products which, by extraordinary coincidence, are only met by locally produced goods. Perhaps the most notorious non-tariff barrier in recent commercial history was imposed by the French in 1982 when they insisted that all imports of video tape recorders should pass through Poitiers, a tiny inland customs post that could handle less than a fifth of the amount of video tape recorders that were previously being imported into France from Japan.

NOT IN MY BACK YARD
Jargon to describe the reaction of the individual to a decision by society that something distasteful must be done. Not in my back yard (NIMBY) is particularly prevalent in environmental issues where all governments can agree that waste must be treated in a particular way, and they can also all agree that it must be NIMBY.

O

OCR
See OPTICAL CHARACTER RECOGNITION.

OFF-THE-SHELF
The opposite of CUSTOM-MADE, a standard item resulting from MASS PRODUCTION with no special features for the individual customer.

An off-the-shelf COMPANY is one that is bought with its legal existence established (it has articles of association and a memorandum), but which has either never carried on any business or has stopped doing business, that is, is dormant. Many businesses are started by an entrepreneur buying an off-the-shelf company.

OFFICE AUTOMATION
The introduction of computers, FAX machines and sophisticated telecommunications equipment into offices. Automation of the office was expected to reduce the need for human LABOUR in the same way as earlier automation of the FACTORY had done, but it seems to have increased the number of office jobs rather than reduced them.

A photocopier is a machine that can reproduce human error flawlessly.

Anon

OFFSHORE
Places which set out to attract foreign-currency financial business by creating a fiscally and legally attractive environment are known as offshore centres. Most of them are on small, warm islands. The definition is somewhat arbitrary, however, since it can embrace the whole of deeply onshore Switzerland.

The best-known offshore centres are members of the Offshore Group of Banking Supervisors. There are 19 of them:

Aruba, Bahamas, Bahrain, Barbados, Bermuda, Cayman Islands, Cyprus, Gibraltar, Guernsey,

Hong Kong, Isle of Man, Jersey, Lebanon, Malta
Mauritius, Netherlands Antilles, Panama, Singapore, Vanuatu.

They have all endorsed the principle that they
should try to prevent the banking system from
being used for the purposes of money launder-
ing. Endorsing a principle, however, is very different from preventing a practice.

OLIGOPOLY
The CONTROL of an industry by a few producers.
Oligopolies can be found in many industries and
can behave like a MONOPOLY, just as the major oil-
producing countries do through OPEC. On the other
hand they can be fiercely competitive, like Procter
& Gamble and Unilever. Between them they dominate the world production of washing powders, yet
every twitch of one makes the other twitch too.

ON-LINE/OFF-LINE
On-line means having access to a remote location
from a COMPUTER via a communications link such
as a telephone line, and it is in real time. Off-line
means that the work is done at a remote location
and is only entered on to the central computer
periodically, either by downloading from a telephone line or by tape or disk, and therefore this
is not in real time.

OPEC
See ORGANISATION OF PETROLEUM EXPORTING
COUNTRIES.

OPEN PLAN
A form of office design in which there are no
dividing walls breaking up the space into separate individual offices. Useful in particular circumstances – in newspaper editorial offices, for
example, where it is efficient for everybody to
hear what everybody else is doing – open-plan
design was a fashion that was taken to extremes.
It was often socially divisive. Senior managers
remained isolated in individual cubicles, while the
rest milled around harbouring their grievances.

O

Many open-plan offices were subsequently altered to give individuals more privacy, and to cut down on noise.

OPERATIONS MANAGEMENT
The management of the production systems of a manufacturing business. The expression has extended to the management of the systems of service industries (like banking) since the skills required for both have been found to be similar.

Operations management has traditionally been on the sidelines of corporate decision-making. Once decisions have been made on where to site plant and machinery (and how far to automate the process), it has been assumed that there is little more to be done. That is a view of operations management as being like flying a jumbo jet across the Atlantic: a question of using the auto-pilot.

Companies have come to realise that operations management can be more closely integrated with other parts of the business, such as MARKETING and new product development. Then it becomes a competitive weapon rather than a fact of life.

If you don't know where you're going, any road will do.
Old saying

OPPORTUNITY COST
The COST of not doing something; a key concept in business economics, but not the sort of cost recognised by accountants. Business always involves making choices, and decision-making involves the rejection of opportunities as much as the selection of them. Should a COMPANY's resources be allocated to launching an existing product into a new MARKET, or a new product into an existing market? Or should the company just put its money in the bank and lay off a few workers? The opportunity cost is the reward that would have come from the best course of action that the business did not follow.

O

If the choice lies between the production or purchase of two commodities, the value of one is measured by the sacrifice of going without the other.

H.J. Davenport

OPTICAL CHARACTER RECOGNITION

An important breakthrough that could have a significant impact on productivity in a number of businesses. Optical character recognition (OCR) is a technology that enables computers to "read" typescript (and ultimately, perhaps, handwritten script) directly. It thus eliminates the need to re-key material into a computer.

OPTION

A CONTRACT which gives a person the right to buy or sell a commodity, currency or security within a given period of time (usually anything up to nine months) at an agreed price, called the striking price. The buyer of the contract pays a small premium for the right to exercise the option.

An option to buy is called a "call option", because the holder of the option has the right to call for the commodity (or whatever) from the taker of the option.

An option to sell is called a "put option", because the holder has the right to put the commodity to the taker at the agreed price.

Options give industry and commerce the chance to fix an advance price for the RAW MATERIALS, currency or financial instruments that they might need. The people who buy their options are usually speculators hoping to make a significant gain from price changes.

There are a growing number of secondary markets where options can be traded between the time that the contract is made and the time that it matures. These give speculators the LIQUIDITY they like to have.

This type of option should be distinguished from a stock option, which is the right given by companies to key employees to buy some of the

COMPANY's shares at a favourable price. Stock options are given as an INCENTIVE to attract and retain key employees. They cannot be traded.

ORGANISATION OF PETROLEUM EXPORTING COUNTRIES

Founded in 1960 to represent the interests of the main oil-exporting nations in their dealings with the major oil companies, the Organisation of Petroleum Exporting Countries (OPEC) is the only really successful primary-product CARTEL. It controls over half of the world's traded oil.

ORGANISED LABOUR

Workers who have organised themselves into TRADE UNIONS in order to use the power of COLLECTIVE BARGAINING in negotiations with their employers.

OTC

See OVER THE COUNTER.

OUTPLACEMENT

Assistance given by an employer to an employee who is being dismissed. The service is often provided by specialist outplacement agencies whose main task is to find the employee a new job. The agency may also give financial advice, counselling to the dismissed employee's family, and tips on how to handle job interviews or to fill in a CV.

OUTWORKER

A person who carries out part of an industrial process for a large corporation from their own home or workshop. Outworkers are usually paid at PIECE RATES according to the quantity of goods that they produce.

Outworkers are at least as old as the INDUSTRIAL REVOLUTION. Early textile factories in England relied heavily on women putting together garments in their homes. The system is still popular with the textile industry in developing countries where work is farmed out to homes and to small independent workshops.

The practice has spread into a number of

modern HIGH-TECH industries too. DATA PROCESSING is an operation that lends itself well to outworkers.

OVERHEADS
The costs of a business that cannot be directly attributed to the production of particular items. A manufacturer's overheads may include such things as:

- administration and personnel departments;
- the finance department;
- warehousing services;
- R&D;
- distribution.

OVER THE COUNTER
An over-the-counter (OTC) market is an informal STOCKMARKET trading shares that are not listed on a main stock exchange.

OVERTIME
Work done by employees in hours that stretch beyond the time that has been agreed with their employer. Overtime is usually paid at a higher rate than normal working hours. Thus, "time and a half" means the rate for normal hours plus 50%; "double time" means twice the normal rate.

OVERTRADING
The price of too rapid, and too early a success. The process of increasing TURNOVER to a level where it is too large to be supported by the other aspects of the business, in particular its WORKING CAPITAL. An over-rapid increase in turnover leaves a COMPANY vulnerable because it has to finance high levels of stocks (to meet the strong demand) as well as high levels of debt (from its rapid growth in sales). This can leave it short of cash to pay its own salaries and its creditors; in short, in trouble.

P&L

See PROFIT AND LOSS ACCOUNT.

PARKINSON'S LAW

The title of a book, first published in 1958 and written by a history professor called Cyril Northcote Parkinson. The book was one of the first about MANAGEMENT to be written in a humorous style, and it made a satirical stab at the self-satisfied behaviour of managers within large organisations. It had a very wide influence and was translated into many languages.

The book contained a number of "laws", of which the most famous is probably: "Work expands to fill the time available for its completion." Allied to this is the principle that: "Expenditure rises to meet income." Others include the observation about management meetings: "The less important the subject; the more animated the discussion."

PARTNERSHIP

Two or more people (the partners) who join together to undertake a business for profit without being incorporated as a COMPANY. Traditionally formed in professions such as accounting and law, partnerships have developed in significantly different ways in different countries. In some countries, for example, a partnership is a recognised legal entity; in others it has no legal existence separate from the existence of the partners themselves.

In general the partners in a partnership will not have the protection of LIMITED LIABILITY, except in the case of a so-called "limited partnership". In this the active (that is executive) partners have unlimited liability, but they also have a number of "limited partners". These partners cannot take part in the MANAGEMENT of the partnership, but their liability is limited to the amount of capital that they have pledged to provide. Limited partnerships are more popular in continental Europe than they are in the UK or the USA. In France they are called *société en commandite*, in Germany *Kommanditgesellschaft*.

P

The partner of my partner is not my partner.
Lawyer's maxim

PAYROLL TAX
A tax imposed on an organisation's paid employees, that is its payroll. Payroll tax is usually levied as a fixed amount per employee, regardless of his or her salary. Its purpose is to encourage business to use LABOUR more efficiently and to become more CAPITAL-INTENSIVE. However, if it merely leaves more people unemployed, it may cost more (in unemployment benefit) than it raises.

PC
See COMPUTER.

If hard work were such a wonderful thing, surely the rich would have kept it to themselves?
Lane Kirkland, president, AFL-CIO

P/E RATIO
See PRICE/EARNINGS RATIO.

PERFORMANCE
How do you compare the performance of one COMPANY with that of another? The short answer is "you cannot", because there is no one single measure that embraces all the goals that a company has. It is not like a high-jumper, whose only aim is to jump higher.

There are a number of measures, however, which in combination provide a close proxy.

- Net sales growth.
- Operating/trading PROFIT growth.
- Operating margins.
- INTEREST COVER.
- Earnings growth.
- RETURN ON CAPITAL.
- PRICE/EARNINGS RATIO (for quoted companies).
- ADDED VALUE.

PERSONAL IDENTIFICATION NUMBER

The series of digits by which bank teller machines recognise individual customers. The personal identification number (PIN) is a sort of "pass number", in contrast to the "password" favoured by the designers of COMPUTER security systems.

PERSONALITY TEST

A method of quickly assessing the character of new recruits. Personality tests have declined in popularity as employers have realised that their usefulness in predicting behaviour is limited, although few ever believed that a complete personality could be revealed in five responses to a smudge of ink.

Some firms do still use techniques like graphology to help them assess the suitability of candidates for jobs.

PERSONNEL MANAGEMENT

The job of developing employees within a COMPANY so that they make the maximum contribution to its success. This includes a range of tasks such as:

- recruitment and selection of new staff;
- TRAINING of new and existing staff;
- defining terms and conditions of employment;
- wage negotiations.

Whereas personnel management used to be concerned mostly with the welfare of employees as individuals, it has recently become more concerned with the MOTIVATION and structure of employees as a group. (See also HUMAN-RESOURCES MANAGEMENT.)

A personnel man with his arm around an employee is like a treasurer with his hand in the till.
Robert Townsend

THE PETER PRINCIPLE

The principle that every man or woman eventually rises to his or her level of incompetence.

First enunciated by Laurence J. Peter in a book published in 1969, the principle (also known as "cream rises until it sours") has become so embedded in MANAGEMENT discussion that it obviously strikes at something deeply felt.

Managers are presumed to be promoted whenever they do jobs competently. They stop being promoted when their "final promotion" takes them to a job that they do incompetently.

Thus Peter's corollary says that "in time, every post tends to be occupied by an employee who is incompetent to carry out its duties". Therefore companies are only kept alive because work is being done by those who have yet to reach their level of incompetence.

Peter revelled in the ailments of those who had obtained their final promotion. They included the following.

- **Galloping phonophilia.** The use of two or more phones to keep in touch with subordinates.
- **Papyrophobia.** Obsessive clearing of the desk.
- **Fileophilia.** The frequent opening of new files.

He recommended that managers demonstrate "creative incompetence" in order to avoid making that final promotion. One example he gave was of the successful manager who avoided promotion by occasionally parking in the space reserved for the COMPANY'S CHAIRMAN.

A variation on the Peter Principle, called the Paula Principle, says that women always stay below their level of incompetence, because they hold back from promotion.

PICKET

An employee who, as part of an industrial dispute, stands at the entrance to the employer's place of business and tries to persuade other employees not to go to work. A picket also tries to persuade suppliers not to deliver, and customers not to buy. Within certain limits, peaceful picketing is legal.

When somebody pickets somebody else's place of business it is called "secondary picketing", which is against the law in most countries.

PIE CHART

A popular way of presenting corporate statistics so that they can be easily understood by the average reader. The whole of a COMPANY's sales, say, are represented by a whole pie. Slices of the pie can then be cut to represent sub-groups of the total sales: either sales broken down by different products, or by geographical region.

PIECE RATE

A method of rewarding workers based on the number of units that they produce. It differs from the more common way of paying employees according to the number of hours they work.

On occasions the two methods of rewarding LABOUR are combined. Workers receive a MINIMUM WAGE which is topped up by a commission that related to the amount of goods (above a minimum) that they sell or produce. Such a combination is a common way of rewarding salesmen.

PIN

See PERSONAL IDENTIFICATION NUMBER.

PLANT AND EQUIPMENT

A commonly used general expression for everything that is required to carry on an industrial process (tools, machines, robots, and so on) other than the buildings, the people, and the fixtures and fittings (air-conditioning systems, and so on).

POINT OF SALE

The place where the customer finally gets together with the product (or service) and a sale is made. Originally a point of sale was a retail shop, but with the introduction of more sophisticated retailing methods it has also come to mean a single check-out counter at a supermarket, or a through-the-wall bank teller (an electronic point of sale).

PORTFOLIO

A collection of SECURITIES (shares or bonds) from

a disparate bunch of companies.

• **Portfolio investment.** The practice of spreading an investor's funds across a wide range of shares to reduce the risk from any one COMPANY or industry.

• **Portfolio MANAGEMENT.** A way of managing a company as if it were a series of discrete bits, each to be considered as a separate part of a portfolio. Portfolio management has been somewhat pushed aside by the fashion for things "holistic", that is, things considered as a whole.

Also a collection of a person's artistic or graphic work; hence a designer may ask if you want to see his or her portfolio.

PORTFOLIO WORK
A way of describing the work of the self-employed specialist who works in a number (a portfolio) of different areas. Some of these may be highly paid, while others give a different sort of reward. For example, someone may work as a COMPUTER consultant, a teacher and a part-time social worker. Portfolio work is expected to increase as lifetime careers with a single employer become rarer.

POSITIONING
The attempt by marketers to define a distinct set of characteristics that differentiate a product or service from its competitors. This is a more subtle process than finding a USP. For example, the positioning of the car-hire firm Avis was firmly behind the market leader Hertz. So Avis made a virtue out of being number two with the slogan: "We're Number Two. We Try Harder". Such a slogan could not be said to describe a USP.

PR
See PUBLIC RELATIONS.

PREFERENTIAL CREDITOR
A CREDITOR who is owed money by a COMPANY in

LIQUIDATION, but who has the right to more favourable treatment than other creditors. Such preferential treatment is given to:

- those with a CHARGE on the company's ASSETS;
- unpaid tax collectors;
- wages and salaries, up to a certain limit.

PRESENTATION

If you want to sell your business plan to the board or a new product to a customer, it is essential to present it well. Verbal presentation must be confident, convincing and articulate. Documents must be clearly written, contain all the necessary information and look professional. A good idea can be lost without good presentation of it.

PRICE/EARNINGS RATIO

The ratio of a COMPANY's stockmarket price (P) to its earnings (E). The P/E ratio is a very closely watched figure among stockbrokers and investment bankers. It is supposed to give some indication of whether a company's shares are undervalued or overvalued.

The P/E ratio compares a company's STOCKMARKET VALUE (that is, its number of shares multiplied by its share price) with its latest annual after-tax profits. Put that the other way round, and the ratio is a measure of how many years it would take an investor get their money back if the company kept profits constant and distributed them all every year. Some hot stocks of the 1980s had P/E ratios of over 30, on the assumption that their profits were going to double or treble over the next few years; in other words they were not going to stay constant.

PRICING

The difficult task of determining the price of a product. A careful calculation of costs can put a floor to that price, but what should be the profit margin added on top? To some extent it will be determined by COMPETITION, but it will also be determined by the costs of distribution, by the POSITIONING of the product, and by the economies of scale that can be reaped by selling larger volumes.

PRINT-OUT

The printed-on-paper version of electronic COMPUTER data. Early machines for producing print-outs were called "daisy-wheel printers". They had a wheel with sprockets which channelled suitably perforated paper in front of the printing head and ribbon. New computer-printing technology (using little jets of ink rather than carbon ribbons) may make the daisy wheel obsolescent.

PRIVATE SECTOR

The private sector is that part of business owned by private individuals; that is, not owned or run by government. PRIVATISATION switches a company from the PUBLIC SECTOR to the private sector.

The private sector is a bit like private education in the UK, confusingly full of "public" institutions: public schools in the case of education; public companies in the case of the private sector.

PRIVATISATION

The process of selling off the shares in a state-owned business to the PRIVATE SECTOR. Following the gospel of Mrs Thatcher in the early 1980s, many countries were converted to privatisation. However, all too rapidly they came up against the privatiser's dilemma: the fact that the businesses the state most wants to sell are those that the private sector least wants to buy, unless sold as a near MONOPOLY.

Privatisation is seen as a way of injecting COMPETITION and entrepreneurship into fossilised state-owned monopolies. Whatever it is, it is certainly not an overnight cure. A utility employing hundreds of thousands of people does not become dashing and dynamic overnight because some pieces of paper change hands. The MANAGEMENT's frame of mind has to change too.

PRODUCT DEVELOPMENT

Something all companies need to do if they are to be successful. All products have a useful or finite life, so new products must be developed to replace dying ones.

The Economist's marketing department lists ten points to consider when embarking on a new project or product.

❒ Current situation: where are you now?
❒ Objectives: where do you want to be?
❒ Competition: who else wants to be there?
❒ Feasibility: can you realistically get there?
❒ Method: how will you get there?
❒ Resources: what do you need to help you get there?
❒ Time-scale: how long will it take to get there?
❒ Fall-back positions: what happens if you get delayed or sidetracked?
❒ Threats and opportunities: what might stop you or help you?
❒ Longer-term plans: what do you do after you've got there?

Finally, draw all these together in a plan or a map to work from.

PRODUCT LIABILITY
The principle that a manufacturer has to pay for damage that occurs as a result of somebody using its products. In the USA product liability awards in the courts can be enormous. In the EUROPEAN COMMUNITY a DIRECTIVE on product liability should soon raise awards and harmonise practice throughout the EC.

PRODUCTION LINE
See ASSEMBLY LINE.

PRODUCTIVITY
One of those common or garden business words that has been taken over by economists and given a very precise meaning: the output produced in a stated period of time by each unit of any of the three factors of production (land, LABOUR and CAPITAL). For example:

- the number of tons of wheat produced per year by an acre of land (land productivity);
- the number of widgets manufactured by one worker in a widget factory in a year (the productivity of labour, and the easiest to measure); or
- (less commonly) the money earned on each dollar invested for a year (the productivity of capital).

PROFIT

To accountants, it is the excess of a COMPANY's revenues over its costs, as calculated in the PROFIT AND LOSS ACCOUNT. If a company's costs exceed its revenues for a period then it has made a loss.

To economists, profit is the reward to entrepreneurs for taking the risks of doing business: what is left from the price of goods when rewards have been paid to the factors of production, such as salaries to LABOUR, rent for land and interest on CAPITAL.

The accountants' profit is far from being very precise. Whenever two accountants look at one company's books they find three profits.

Their uncertainty increases because of the many different ways of using the word profit.

- **After-tax profit.** The gross profit less tax.
- **Attributable profit.** Profit that can be attributed to a particular division or department of an organisation.
- **Gross profit.** The profit before the deduction of things like tax and exceptional payments.
- **MONOPOLY profit.** The exceptional profit that a firm can earn if it has a monopoly in a MARKET.
- **Net profit.** The gross profit less tax and other exceptional payments.
- **Paper profit.** A profit that has been earned but not yet realised, like that from the rise in the SHARE price of a company whose shares an investor has not yet sold.
- **Retained profit.** The profit that is left to the company after absolutely everything else has been paid.

> *What profiteth it a man if he gain the whole world, yet lose his own soul?*
> The Bible

- **Windfall profit.** An unexpected profit that suddenly appears from nowhere (through a DEVALUATION, perhaps, or the death of Uncle Tom).

> *It is not the aim of Marks and Spencer to make more money than is prudent.*
> Lord Rayner, when chairman

PROFIT AND LOSS ACCOUNT

The P&L account, widely referred to in the USA as the income statement, is one of the two main financial statements to be shown in a COMPANY's ANNUAL REPORT. The other is the BALANCE SHEET. While the balance sheet takes a snapshot of a company's financial condition on the last day of its financial year, the profit and loss account is a record of the company's revenues and expenses during the year.

Managers produce frequent P&L statements for their own internal purposes, but the only legal requirement is for an audited account to be produced once a year.

P&L accounts differ from country to country in the amount of detail that they show. Most of the differences lie in footnotes which increasingly dwarf the accounts themselves.

> *The word "love" is never mentioned in big business.*
> Anita Roddick, founder of Body Shop

PROFIT CENTRE

A self-contained part of an organisation that is accountable for its own profits and losses. This is not as straightforward as it sounds. In order to be accountable it has to work out the costs and revenues associated with the goods and services that it buys and sells from other parts of the organisation. That includes things like payroll services, and the services of the COMPANY's tea lady.

PROFIT MARGIN
See MARGIN.

PROFIT SHARING
An arrangement between the employees and the owners of a business whereby the employees receive an agreed amount of the COMPANY's PROFIT to be shared among themselves. Such schemes sound splendid in theory, a direct financial INCENTIVE for MANAGEMENT to maximise the reward to EQUITY.

In practice, profit-sharing schemes fall foul of all sorts of little jealousies. One of the most common is between those departments which know they made the biggest contribution to profits, and those departments which do not believe the figures.

> *The idea of making workers share in profits is a very attractive one and it would seem that it is from there that harmony between capital and labour should come. But the practical formula for such sharing has not yet been found.*
> Henri Fayol

PROFITABILITY
The ability of a COMPANY to make profits, often loosely used as a synonym for profits themselves: "The company's profitability was high last year", to wit, "it made a lot of profit".

There is an important distinction between PROFIT and profitability: a company that sets out to maximise its profit is not going to maximise its profitability. Maximum profits are obtained when a company is producing at the MARGIN, when the COST of the last unit of output was just less than its revenue. Maximum profitability occurs long before that, when the difference between cost and revenue is a maximum.

P

PROGRAM

The series of steps taken by a COMPUTER to solve a particular problem. The person who feeds a computer with the raw data on which the program is to work is called a computer programmer.

PROTECTIONISM

Any obstacle to trade that attempts to put a domestic producer at an advantage vis-à-vis its foreign competitors (see TARIFF). The experience of many countries has shown that protectionism may be helpful to local industry in the short term, but in the long term it cuts them off from progress and change. It can leave local firms as vulnerable as the dodo when the protectionism is removed.

American-made parts now constitute a smaller portion of the top models of General Motors, Ford and Chrysler than they do of Honda's top models.

PROVISION

What nuts are to squirrels, provisions are to accountants: money put aside out of the harvest of current profits to be consumed in the future.

Provisions come in two shapes: general and specific. Specific provisions are set aside against future LIABILITIES that can be determined with a reasonable degree of accuracy and with a reasonable degree of certainty that they will happen. General provisions are set aside against nothing more definite than past experience of the general level of the industry's liabilities.

PUBLIC COMPANY

A COMPANY that is allowed to market its SECURITIES, usually through a stock exchange.

The precise nature of public and private companies differs from country to country. In the USA a public company is one which is registered with the SECURITIES AND EXCHANGE COMMISSION. In Europe there are a number of near-equivalent names and abbreviations.

France	Société à responsabilité limitée (SARL)	Société anonyme (SA)
Germany	Gesellschaft mit beschränkter Haftung (GmbH)	Aktien-gesellschaft (AG)
Italy	Società a responsabilità limitata (SRL)	Società per azioni (SPA)
Netherlands	Besloten vennootschap (BV)	Naamloze vennootschap (NV)
Spain	Sociedad de responsabilidad limitada (SRL)	Sociedad anónima (SA)
UK	Private company	Public limited company (PLC)

PUBLIC PROCUREMENT

The way in which national governments and PUB-LIC-SECTOR bodies place orders for large-scale contracts like building dams, making soldiers' boots, or building an electricity grid. There are several peculiar features about these contracts.

• Because of their size, firms often get together as a CONSORTIUM in order to be big enough to bid for them.

• So big are the numbers that firms can easily end up working for just one customer (a single government department). That is a monopsony (where there is a single buyer), as opposed to a MONOPOLY (where there is a single supplier), and leaves the firm exposed to high risks.

• Governments looking at tenders for public procurement contracts have traditionally favoured their own national firms. The EUROPEAN COMMUNI-TY is trying to open up public procurement so that firms from anywhere within the Community get equal treatment with national firms.

PUBLIC RELATIONS

The art of presenting an organisation's views and interests in as favourable a light as possible to its many different constituencies: investors, customers, employees, legislators, environmentalists, and so on. Some companies employ outside public relations (PR) consultants; others employ full-time specialists in-house. The very largest companies often use a combination of both.

The traditional way to reach external audiences is through the media – the press, television and radio – via press releases, press conferences, and interviews with key people in the organisation. Journalists and public-relations managers have a love/hate relationship: the information that the PR manager wants to give is rarely the information that the journalist wants to receive.

Public relations within organisations, via in-house magazines, is a rapidly growing aspect of the business. So too is investor relations, which is concerned with the relationship between a PUBLIC COMPANY and its large (and constantly changing) group of shareholders.

PUBLIC SECTOR

That part of a nation's economy that is owned and run by government (the opposite of PRIVATE SECTOR). In a communist country virtually the whole of the economy is in the public sector. When there is a substantial private sector as well, an economy is said to be "mixed". There is no economy with no public sector.

PURCHASING POWER

The capacity of CONSUMERS to spend money on goods and services. Hence the amount of goods and services that consumers can buy with a given unit of currency.

Purchasing power parity (PPP) is the EXCHANGE RATE between two currencies calculated according to how many units of each currency are required to buy an identical basket of goods and services in each currency's country.

QUALITY CONTROL

The testing of a sample of products before they are shipped to a buyer in order to see if they are of the specified quality. A certain tolerance of error may be acceptable in the sample (say, 5%). Above that buyers will demand further checks. If the faults are large and extensive they can refuse to take the goods.

It is difficult for companies that are importing goods from far away to carry out rigorous quality-control checks, but there are firms that specialise in carrying out checks on behalf of buyers. By far the biggest in this business is a Swiss firm called SGS, Société Générale de Surveillance.

Nowadays more and more companies realise that it is pointless to learn at the end of the production process – just before they are due to take delivery – that their goods are no good. It is much better for quality control to begin at the moment when the very first step in the production process is taken.

> *Quality is remembered long after the price is forgotten.*
> Gucci slogan

QUORUM

The minimum number of people required to hold an official meeting (such as a COMPANY BOARD meeting). If a quorum is not present then any decisions taken at the meeting are invalid.

QUOTED COMPANY

A COMPANY whose shares are traded on a stock exchange. A company joins the list of other companies "listed" on the stock exchange when dealers on the floor of the exchange "quote" a price for its shares, a price at which they are prepared to trade in those shares.

R

R&D

See RESEARCH AND DEVELOPMENT.

RAT RACE

A colloquial expression for the perpetual struggle of individuals to be successful in their working lives. What people look forward to being rid of when they retire. Based on the curious notion that anything to do with the long-tailed rodent is unpleasant. For example, people who carry on working during a STRIKE are referred to as "rats" when they are not being referred to as "scabs".

RATE OF RETURN

The reward from an investment expressed as a percentage of the original investment. The reward includes both CAPITAL gain and income. This provides a crude way of comparing the relative attractions of a number of investments. Is it more rewarding to place $10,000 today in an interest-earning bank account and leave it there for five years, or to give it to your nephew for his new Guatemalan fast-food business which he hopes to sell to a PUBLIC COMPANY in five years' time?

The rate of return is a crude method of comparison because it takes no account of time. Most of the reward from the fast-food business will come as capital gain in five years' time. The reward from the bank is the interest paid at regular intervals throughout the five years.

One method of trying to take account of time in such calculations is called discounted CASH FLOW. It reduces all the elements of the reward to their NET PRESENT VALUE; what they would be worth if they were to be received in cash today. Then in any calculation of rates of return, apples are properly being added to apples.

Note also that the rate of return takes no account of differing degrees of certainty. The bank interest is almost as safe as houses; the nephew's prospective capital gain is not.

RATIONALISATION

Frequently given as a sound reason for redundancies:

"As part of a rationalisation the COMPANY is laying off 2,000 machinists." Yet rationalisation – a major reorganisation of a company's structure to improve efficiency – can be an admission that MANAGEMENT got it wrong last time they reorganised things. The irrationality of rationalisation is that it usually gives the BLUE-COLLAR WORKER the boot while allowing management to have another go.

RAW MATERIALS
The most primitive inputs into an industrial process. In many cases these are minerals or agricultural materials that have come straight from the ground.

Sometimes they are semi-processed materials. Silicon chips are the raw material of the COMPUTER industry, for example.

RECEIVER
Somebody appointed by a court to "receive" a troubled COMPANY's ASSETS on behalf of its DEBENTURE holders (usually its bankers). Receivers, normally accountants or solicitors, are presented with an all-or-nothing choice. Either they try to get the bank's money back by running the company for a while in the hope of turning it round. Or, the more popular and quicker option, they liquidate the company straightaway.

Legal procedures like CHAPTER 11 and ADMINISTRATION aim to adjust the balance in such situations in favour of creditors other than debenture holders.

RECONCILE
To make a COMPANY's various sets of books agree with each other and be mutually consistent. To do so, you may also have to reconcile yourself to a touch of fantasy.

RECRUITMENT
The business of identifying and selecting new employees, often from a particular group of the population as in "graduate recruitment".

RECYCLING

The art of re-using materials that would otherwise be thrown away. Although most publicity on recycling is focused on attempts to re-use household waste such as paper, glass or aluminium, the majority of recycling is done in industry. Worthwhile savings can be made from retrieving expensive chemicals, and from recycling paper in large offices.

Here are some tips for setting up a recycling scheme in an office (taken from *The Green Consumer Guide*, John Elkington and Julia Hailes, Gollancz, 1988).

- ❑ Appoint an enthusiastic co-ordinator.
- ❑ Find a local wastepaper merchant who will collect the waste.
- ❑ Find suitable storage space; 2 square metres per 1,000 square metres of office space is suggested.
- ❑ Set up a system of colour-coded bins for different types of paper.
- ❑ Constantly monitor the system's performance and look for ways to improve it.

REDUNDANCY

The sad state of being no longer needed by an employer. Between 1982 and 1985 the US firm General Electric reduced its workforce of 400,000 by 100,000, yet its TURNOVER increased during the period. The 100,000 were made redundant because they were literally redundant.

Employees who are made redundant differ from employees who are sacked.

- Redundancy occurs through no fault of the individual employee; sacking can only occur after there has been unreasonable behaviour by an employee.
- Employees who are made redundant may have a legal right to certain redundancy payments, usually dependent on their length of service.

Here are some guidelines to follow when making someone redundant.

❐ Give as much notice to the employee as possible.
❐ Look for suitable redeployment opportunities.
❐ Ensure that if procedures exist they are followed.
❐ Consider the possibility of OUTPLACEMENT counselling.
❐ Ensure that the employee knows about and receives all relevant benefits.
❐ Keep written records at all stages of the redundancy process.

RELOCATION

Moving elsewhere. Most managers who join a large organisation do not expect to live in one place for the whole of their careers. They may be relocated as individuals to another part of their firm in another part of the country (or, indeed, in another country). Or the part of the firm that they work for may itself be relocated to another part of the country (where LABOUR is cheaper or where the firm is closer to important new markets). In very large firms, relocating employees around the world can call for the highest logistical skills.

REPLACEMENT COST

The COST of replacing an asset today. Replacement-cost accounting attempts to draw up a COMPANY'S ACCOUNTS using replacement cost as the basis for valuing all the company's ASSETS. So all machinery and buildings are valued at the price it would cost to buy them today, not the price at which they were bought originally.

The alternative, HISTORIC-COST accounting, is more objective and simpler, but (perhaps) theoretically less pure.

Replacement-cost accounting has been most popular in the Netherlands, and for many years the electronics firm Philips used to produce an additional set of replacement-cost accounts.

R

RESEARCH AND DEVELOPMENT

The crucial part of any modern industry, in which scientists and designers search for new products and for new ways of developing existing products. Research refers to the work of pure scientists; chemists and engineers, for example. Development is more concerned with creating marketable products out of the findings of the researchers.

Expenditure on research and development (R&D) does not bring immediate returns. Scientists and their laboratories are working for future profits. In most fields it takes 10–20 years from the dawning of an idea to its full commercial MARKETING. That is at least twice as long as the average lifespan of a chief executive.

Some industries are more dependent on R&D than others. The pharmaceutical industry's success is closely related to the ability of white-coated scientists to come up with new drugs in their laboratories. It can cost $50m and more in R&D to produce an effective new drug, but success is well rewarded. The discovery of the anti-ulcer drug Zantac completely transformed the fortunes of Glaxo.

Japanese companies are famous for their development rather than their research. It is sometimes assumed that this is a rather inferior skill, but a reassessment of the VALUE of development is long overdue. Great breakthroughs in research are rare; the COMPANY that continually develops its existing products is more assured of a long and successful future.

At 3M every scientist devotes 15% of his or her time to projects of his or her own choice.

RESERVES

Amounts of money that are set aside out of profits. The distinction between reserves and provisions is not always clear. Reserves are set aside voluntarily out of profits (and belong to the

COMPANY's shareholders), provisions are set aside as a prudent bit of accounting to cover an expected future liability (or future decrease in the VALUE of an asset, which is the same thing). The value of the shareholders' stake in a company is its CAPITAL plus its reserves.

RESTRICTIVE PRACTICES

Any business practice that restricts free COMPETITION. In free-market economies governments keep a close eye on such practices. Restrictive practices come in many forms. They can be agreements between manufacturers (and distributors) to sell products or services at a fixed price (known as resale price maintenance). Such agreements exist in Europe, for example, in book retailing. Restrictive practices are also common (though less so than they once were) among the so-called professions.

MANAGEMENT and TRADE UNIONS sometimes collude in restrictive practices by deciding that, for example, two people are required to do a particular job regardless of the fact that advances in technology mean that it can be done perfectly well by one person.

It is often difficult to tell the difference between perfect competition and a restrictive practice. For example, do banks charge exactly the same for their various services because they collude in fixing their prices? Or do they charge the same because competition between them is so perfect that no one of them can afford to be out of line with the others?

RETURN ON CAPITAL

The RATE OF RETURN on CAPITAL; in particular, the relationship between the net PROFIT of a business and the paid-up SHARE capital of the business.

This is a measure whereby shareholders can find out if their money would have been better employed in a bank, but it is a measure to be wary of: there are almost as many ways of calculating profit as there are of calculating capital.

RETURN ON SALES
The relationship between sales (TURNOVER) and
PROFIT. (See MARGIN.)

RIGHTS ISSUE
An offer of new shares for cash to existing shareholders in proportion to the size of their stake in
the COMPANY. For example, a one-for-three rights
issue entitles every holder of three shares to buy
one more at a special price.

Rights issues are popular in good times, as a
"cheap" way to fund new investment or to pay
for mergers and acquisitions. They are also popular in bad times, to replace expensive debt or to
take advantage of bargain acquisitions.

Their main disadvantages are as follows.

• It is a long time before the issuing company
lays its hands on the cash.
• Since they are usually offered at a DISCOUNT,
rights issues raise less cash than the face VALUE of
the shares.
• They are administratively tricky if the issuing
company has a particularly large number of
shareholders.

RISK
The amount that stands to be lost by a certain
action or investment. This may be measured in
monetary terms: "He risked thousands on that
research"; or in non-monetary terms: "He risked
his reputation by employing Joe Bloggs." The
main calculation in all business is the set-off
between risk and reward. Is the degree of risk
involved in doing something justified by the
potential reward?

ROBOTICS
The development of machines (called robots) to
do work formerly done by humans. The motor
industry in particular uses robots extensively
throughout the manufacturing process. Fiat is
probably the world's biggest manufacturer of
robots.

R

ROYALTIES
Money paid to somebody else for the use of certain types of property. For example:

• to the owner of land for the right to extract minerals from the land;
• to authors for the right to publish their books; or
• to the owner of a patent for use of the thing patented.

S

SALARY SCALE

A table which shows the salaries paid to employees at different levels (grades) in an organisation. The scale may define salaries within a particular grade according to rank, length of service, special skills (such as languages), and time spent in the grade.

Few organisations are sufficiently rigid to find salary scales as useful as they are to civil servants, but companies have to make some sort of evaluation of different jobs within their organisation, and salary scales are simply a quantification of that process.

Salaries for some jobs can be largely determined by the general LABOUR MARKET, but these are the commodity-type jobs in computing and BOOK-KEEPING, for example. For the bespoke jobs, whose VALUE lies largely in experience and knowledge of a particular firm, salary scales are almost unavoidable.

One problem with salary scales: who sets the scales for the people who set the scales? Is it just coincidence that the salaries of executive directors and chief executives (who usually set the scales) so often seem to fly right off the top of the scales that they set?

That's the American way. If little kids don't aspire to make money like I did, what the hell good is this country?

Lee Iacocca, when asked how he reconciled his $20.6m compensation from Chrysler in 1986 with Chrysler's cuts in pay for other employees

---

SALES

See TURNOVER.

SALE AND LEASEBACK

An agreement between a business and a property investor whereby the business sells land or buildings that it owns to the investor, and then immediately leases them back (see LEASING). The business receives a large CAPITAL sum and, in return, starts paying regular rent to the investor.

Such agreements release the capital tied up in business premises, freeing it for more productive purposes. Sale and leaseback deals are attractive to speculators who buy companies solely for their idle property. The property is sold and leased back, and the cash can then be used to buy another bigger company in a similar position, and so on, ad infinitum.

SBU
See STRATEGIC BUSINESS UNIT.

SEC
See SECURITIES AND EXCHANGE COMMISSION.

SECURITIES
Originally the documents that gave evidence of the ownership of investments like shares or bonds. Now it has come to mean the investments themselves: "The art MARKET last year was dead, but securities had a whale of a time."

Since security is also the backing given by a borrower to a lender for a loan (property in the case of a mortgage), some prefer the word "security" not to be used to refer to shares. Ironically, shareholders are the one type of investor with absolutely no security to back the securities they have bought, or, "the only security they have is their security".

SECURITIES AND EXCHANGE COMMISSION
The powerful policeman of US securities markets. Based in Washington DC, the Securities and Exchange Commission (SEC) relies heavily on disclosure of information to do its job. Public companies have to disclose far more to the SEC than they do anywhere else in the world. Many companies shy away from being a QUOTED COMPANY in the USA for this reason.

SEED MONEY
The very first small investment in a project.

Unlikely to be enough to get the project fully off the ground, but enough to finance, say, a bit of MARKET RESEARCH that will convince a bank to back the project fully.

Everyone lives by selling something.
Robert Louis Stevenson

SEGMENTATION
The categorising of consumers into a number of different segments, each of which has a distinctive feature. The categorising may be done according to basic demographic features, such as age, sex, country of residence, and so on. Or it may be done according to less precise "lifestyle" criteria, such as Yuppies, "baby-boomers", or "empty-nesters".

The purpose of segmentation is to identify more precisely the target MARKET for a particular product or service. Surprisingly few products can genuinely hope to appeal to everybody. Even something like beer is consumed largely by a relatively small number of young males with a very distinctive lifestyle.

SEMICONDUCTOR
A substance (like silicon) that "conducts" an electric current less efficiently than metal, but more efficiently than an insulator (like rubber); that is, a semi-efficient conductor. Such materials are the bedrock of COMPUTER science.

SETTING-UP COST
The COST involved in changing a set of machines from producing one product to producing something else. Most of this cost lies in the amount of time that the machines and the people operating them are idle while the change is taking place.

SEVEN Ss
Seven qualities (each beginning with the letter S) which were identified in a best-selling book (*The*

Art of Japanese Management) as being the areas in which Japanese companies excelled over US companies. The book was written by Richard Pascale and came out a year before the even better selling *In Search of Excellence* by Tom Peters and Robert Waterman. Pascale, Peters and Waterman had all worked together at the management consultants McKinsey where they had gleaned much of the basic research for their respective books.

The Seven Ss were: STRATEGY, structure and systems; style, shared values, skills and staff. The first three were called the hard Ss; the last four the soft Ss. The Japanese made the hard Ss more productive by allying them better with the soft Ss than did western companies.

SHARE

The CAPITAL of most companies is divided into many small parts called shares. "The capital of ABC Inc is divided into 3,000 shares of $4 each." The reward to people who buy shares (shareholders) is an annual DIVIDEND.

There are a number of different types of share, each giving the shareholder a different right over the COMPANY'S ASSETS. The basic share is called an ordinary share. Some variations are as follows.

- **A and B shares.** Common in some continental European countries, but frowned upon in the UK and the USA. These shares carry differential voting rights: A shares, always owned by the general public, have restricted voting rights (and sometimes none at all); B shares, usually owned by the founders and those they favour, have full voting rights.
- **Preference shares.** These are paid a fixed dividend in preference to others, such as the ordinary shareholders.
- **Deferred shares.** These are paid last, after preference and ordinary shareholders have had their bite. They are often held by the company's founders, who then get a big chunk of what is left.

Shareholders' funds
The same as NET WORTH.

Shift
A group of employees who work together for a fixed period of time. Shifts are used in industrial processes where work is required during and beyond the normal working day. This may be because it is expensive to shut down machinery every night, and the product of operating for 24 hours a day can all be sold. Or it may be because the nature of the work (some sorts of retailing, for example) demands that it stretch beyond the standard day.

There are three main patterns of shift work.

• **The double-day shift.** Two eight-hour periods stretching from 6.00am to 10.00pm.
• **Three eight-hour shifts.** Usually called the morning shift, the afternoon shift, and the night (or "graveyard") shift.
• **The part-time shift.** One which takes over in the evenings for a number of hours after the normal day shift has finished work.

Shifts are sometimes rotated, with one shift working an eight-hour day for two weeks before doing the anti-social eight-hour shift through the night for one week. In general, however, shift workers prefer not to be rotated, but then it becomes difficult and expensive to hold a permanent night shift together.

Shifts are often introduced for short periods when demand is exceptionally high; just before the Christmas holidays, for instance.

Shop floor
Literally, the FACTORY floor on which a COMPANY's main production takes place; but also the body of workers who make that production possible, as in "he (she) rose from the shop floor to become managing director".

S

SHRINKAGE

The reduction in stocks or output due to:

- shoplifting,
- the disappearance of goods in transit;
- careless handling; or
- bad workmanship.

A certain percentage of production inevitably disappears in shrinkage, but a careful eye needs to be kept on that percentage. Any sudden change may be because, for example, a thief has joined the COMPANY, or because QUALITY CONTROL has slipped.

SITC

See STANDARD INDUSTRIAL TRADE CLASSIFICATION.

SINGLE MARKET

A programme devised by the European Commission and designed to turn the 12 members of the EUROPEAN COMMUNITY into a true "single market" by the end of 1992. The idea of Europe as a "common market" was always fundamental to the EC, but progress towards that goal was very slow in the 1970s and early 1980s.

The single market programme gave progress a boost, helped greatly by two contemporaneous agreements among the EC member states.

• To accept majority voting among themselves on many issues, instead of the previously required unanimous vote.
• To accept the principle of mutual recognition. That meant nations could say to each other: "I will accept your qualifications (to be an architect, or whatever) if you will accept mine." Previously they had attempted to draw up a set of uniform rules that everybody would accept. Needless to say, that usually proved to be impossible.

The single market programme consisted of almost 300 directives removing various barriers to the free movement of CAPITAL, LABOUR and goods between the 12 member states.

By 1992 a large number of these directives had still to be passed by the European Council of Ministers.

There was an even larger number waiting to be passed into the legislation of individual member states, a necessary process before a DIRECTIVE can have effect.

We all know 1992 is coming. The question is when.

Karl Otto Pohl in 1990, when head of the Bundesbank

SMALL AND MEDIUM-SIZED ENTERPRISES
The lifeblood of a nation's industry; a fact recognised by most governments through special tax rates and through special agencies (such as the Small Business Administration in the USA) set up to provide soft loans and other support services to small and medium-sized enterprises (SMES).

There is one big unanswered question about SMES. Are they such a wonderful thing that a nation with nothing else would beat the pants off Japan? Or are they mere sucker fish, totally dependent on contracts from bigger fish for survival?

SOFTWARE
The opposite of HARDWARE. Those bits of a COMPUTER that are generally invisible; the bundle of electronic messages, for example, that make up a computer PROGRAM, without which hardware is as useless as a rock in Arizona.

SOLE TRADER
If you cannot found a COMPANY, then a PARTNERSHIP will do. If you cannot find a partner, then God bless you. Because you will have to be a sole trader: like small shopkeepers who trade only on their own account. They may have employees, but whatever PROFIT they make at the end of the day is all theirs.

SOURCES AND USES OF FUNDS
An accounting statement showing the cash coming in and the cash going out of a COMPANY during a year; that is the alterations in its WORKING CAPITAL. In some countries such statements are an obligatory part of a company's annual ACCOUNTS.

SPAN OF CONTROL
The optimum number of subordinates over whom a manager can exercise CONTROL. In 1933 a MANAGEMENT consultant called V. Graicunas attempted to demonstrate mathematically that it is impossible to exercise proper control over any more than six.

Most consultants since agree that "it depends on the six". Some chief executives have been found to exercise direct control over more than 20 staff without any apparent loss of efficiency. Others seem to find even one disturbing.

SPECIAL PROMOTION
A MARKETING term for an exceptional offer of a new or revived product. This can come in a number of different guises: for example, it can be in the form of a price DISCOUNT for a limited period of time; or it can consist of a heavily advertised competition giving away the product as prizes; or, more modestly, it can be a special window-display appearing for a while in a conspicuous department store.

Whatever form it takes, a special promotion (if successful) requires that production schedules be temporarily adjusted. Its aim is to create an exceptional level of demand in order to introduce new customers to a product.

SPECIFICATION
The detailed description of an article and the way it is to be produced, given by a buyer to a supplier. Sometimes called "spec": "This sample is not according to spec."

SPOT CHECK
An unannounced random check to see that work

is being done correctly. It can be used as a technique of QUALITY CONTROL, but only as part of a wider system of checking. A spot check may fall on one of the few articles well-produced, or, indeed, on one of the few articles badly produced.

SPREADSHEET
A type of COMPUTER PROGRAM particularly useful in aspects of business such as planning, budgeting or investment APPRAISAL. It enables the user to change one variable in a string of complicated mathematical relationships, and have the computer roll out the effect on all the other variables. Ideal, say, when you have just planned and costed a DIRECT MAIL operation, and the post office comes up with an entirely new price structure.

STAKEHOLDER
This refers to the wide range of "constituencies" that have a "stake" in a corporation's activities. These constituencies range from suppliers to employees to customers to government. They also include shareholders.

At different times in business history, and in different industrial societies, certain stakeholders have gained power and influence at the expense of others. In the UK and the USA the shareholder has been king for some time; the customer a mere incidental. In Japan the situation is exactly the reverse. In both cases there are imbalances between stakeholders which need to be corrected.

STANDARD DEVIATION
A basic statistical measure of the extent to which a series of data spreads out from a central core figure. This is important for managers as a tool to help them judge, for example, how far sales (or interest rates) might rise or fall in future business cycles based on the extent of their deviation from a norm (or "standard") in the past.

STANDARD INDUSTRIAL TRADE CLASSIFICATION
A widely used system of numbering industrial sectors, sub-sectors and individual products.

Particularly useful to government agencies and statisticians, investment analysts and market researchers.

Standard industrial trade classification (SITC) numbers have six digits: the first two indicate the basic industry; the third gives the industry subgroup; the fourth, the specific industry; the fifth, the product class; and the sixth, the individual product.

STANDARDISATION

The process of getting rid of variety. This can apply to a production line on which it is more efficient to produce only two "standardised" products rather than 13 or 30. Or it can apply to an industry (or a group of countries like the EURO-PEAN COMMUNITY) which agree to certain standards that their products must meet.

Such standards may be applied to the dimensions or contents of the products, and may be produced for perfectly sound reasons like safety. They may also be produced for unsound reasons, like the need to find work for idle bureaucrats.

Within the EC the process is more commonly called "harmonisation" (see SINGLE MARKET).

START-UP

A business that is just beginning. "Start-up COST" is the money that such a business needs before it begins to trade.

Those involved in start-ups have four main places to look for such money.

• Their own pockets, or those of family and friends.
• Commercial banks.
• Government funds.
• Venture capital.

STOCK-IN-TRADE

The stock of goods that a COMPANY needs to hold in order to carry on its normal business. These consist of inputs to the various stages of production, and of finished goods held to meet future demand.

Such goods and materials sit idle and cost a business money. In recent years much effort has gone into refining methods of "stock CONTROL" (when to order how much of what) so that stock-in-trade can be kept to a minimum without affecting productivity. Computers have helped a lot; and so too have new Japanese techniques, such as JUST-IN-TIME. (See also INVENTORY.)

STOCK OPTION
See OPTION.

STOCKMARKET
The first stockmarkets were places where farmers met to buy and sell their livestock. They are now more usually markets in stocks and shares. Traditionally stockmarkets had a physical presence in a building called a stock exchange, where traders got together to meet brokers and to deal. Nowadays they increasingly exist in the ether, with deals struck between brokers who rarely take their eyes off a COMPUTER screen. They go even more rarely into a stock exchange.

October. This is one of the peculiarly dangerous months to speculate in stocks. The others are July, January, September, April, November, May, March, June, December, August and February.
Mark Twain

STOCKTAKING
The business of recording and counting the amount of STOCK-IN-TRADE held by a COMPANY. This has to be done at least once a year for the annual ACCOUNTS. But with the help of computerised records of sales and purchases, stocktaking can be a continuous process, with a company able to say at any one moment how much stock it holds. Nevertheless, it will still need to have a physical stocktaking every now and then, if only to check that the goods which its records say are there, really are there.

S

STRATEGIC BUSINESS UNIT

A self-contained part of a business that serves a homogeneous MARKET; that is, bits of business that have been stuck together because they all supply the same sort of customer, and can do so better by being together. A strategic business unit (SBU) can cut right across traditional geographical and functional divisions within an organisation, and has been encouraged by the love affair that industry in most countries has been having recently with its customers.

STRATEGY

A proposal for a course of action that will lead to a defined goal. Strategy has become to business what Andy Warhol was once to movies: "You may not understand it, but you can't afford to stop talking about it."

Strategy has taken over where planning (the corporate fad of the 1960s and 1970s) left off. It involves the whole panoply of techniques whereby a corporation attempts to get from here to there, once it has decided where "there" is.

STRIKE

Strikes started out by being good things. Gold prospectors made lucky strikes in California in 1849. Then they became bad things, occasions when workers refused to work in order to try and force their employers to pay them more. Nowadays such organised withdrawals of LABOUR are more euphemistically referred to as "industrial action".

If industrial workers are taking industrial action when they are not working, one wonders what they are doing when they are working.
Duke of Edinburgh

SUBCONTRACTOR

A COMPANY or individual who agrees to provide goods or services to another company in order to help that company fulfil a CONTRACT it has with a third party. The subcontractor has no contract with the third party.

SUBSIDIARY

A COMPANY which is controlled by another company, called a holding company. In most cases such CONTROL is demonstrated by the holding company owning more than 50% of the subsidiary's shares.

A company may, however, still be a subsidiary if another company owns less than 50% of its shares but controls the composition of its BOARD. A subsidiary of company X is also a subsidiary of any company of which X is, in turn, a subsidiary.

Subsidiary companies matter to:

• accountants, who "consolidate" them with their holding companies; and
• tax inspectors, who want to be sure that there is no TAX EVASION from the inessential shunting of goods between subsidiaries and their holding company.

Big companies are small companies that succeeded.
Robert Townsend

SUBSIDISE

The giving of money, usually by government, to a COMPANY or industry in order to reduce its prices below what they would otherwise be.

Governments subsidise industries for various reasons.

• To save jobs a little longer in declining industries, like steel or shipbuilding.
• As a form of PROTECTIONISM against foreign manufacturers, of things like sugar and apples.
• As a way of cultivating new HIGH-TECH industries which are struggling to survive.
• As a way of ensuring that nationally significant

industries, such as aerospace or weapons, do not die out.

SUNRISE INDUSTRY
A young industry that is growing fast, usually in the HIGH-TECH area. The sort of business that is found in science parks on the edge of towns with technologically advanced universities (for example, near Boston in the USA, Nice in France or Cambridge in the UK).

SUNSET INDUSTRY
An old industry that is dying slowly, often because governments will not allow free-market euthanasia. Such industries are frequently metal-based and found near water-borne transport.

SWAP
Technically an agreement between two parties to swap their debts, so that one meets the interest and CAPITAL payments of the other, and vice versa. Such an arrangement can be useful if, for example, one borrower wants to change the currency of its debt. This might make what it owes match better what it is owed.

SYSTEM
The way in which something organises its own internal procedures, as in COMPUTER system or monetary system. A systems analyst designs programs that make computers perform required tasks. Companies also have systems that need to be redesigned occasionally.

TACTICS

A term borrowed from the military; the means whereby a STRATEGY is to be achieved.

TAKEOVER

The noun, spelt as a single word, as distinct from the verb to take over, spelt as two words. To take over a COMPANY is simply to gain CONTROL of it. A takeover is a formal process of gaining control which, in the case of public companies, involves procedures dictated by the local stock exchange and/or government. A "hostile takeover" is one that is unwelcome to the company being taken over; a "reverse takeover" is one where the company being taken over successfully defends itself by launching a takeover bid for the company that is bidding for it; a case of the biter bit.

Somebody wishing to launch a takeover of a public company makes a bid: an offer to the company's shareholders for their shares. The offer includes a price and a deadline, by which time the shareholders must have rejected or accepted the offer.

The price may either be in cash (a "cash offer"), or in shares and other SECURITIES of the company making the bid (a "paper offer"). In a cash offer the price must be higher than the quoted price of the shares of the company being bid for. Otherwise shareholders will be better off selling their shares on the STOCKMARKET.

With a paper offer shareholders have some complicated calculations to make. The VALUE of the shares that they are being offered will fluctuate. When the brewer Guinness bid for the Scotch-maker Distillers, it offered its own shares to Distillers' shareholders. Guinness then contrived artificially (and illegally) to raise its share price so that it would have to give Distillers' shareholders fewer shares.

There are many more takeovers in English-speaking countries – where shares tend to be widely held – than there are elsewhere. Hostile takeovers are hugely disruptive to both the taker-over and the taken-over, and cases where they are fully justified in the long term are probably few. In the USA merged companies have been found to lose, on average, about 40% of the joint market share of the pre-merged companies.

TARGET PRICE
There are two meanings.

1   The price that a buyer sets a manufacturer for goods whose COST the manfacturer has been asked to estimate.
2   A technical term within the EUROPEAN COMMUNITY's Common Agricultural Policy: the price fixed from time to time by the EC for agricultural goods. It is not a guaranteed price that farmers will get, but an estimate of what would be a fair price for them.

TARIFF
A tax on imported goods, usually expressed as a percentage of the VALUE of the goods. Under a series of so-called "rounds" of the GATT, countries have gradually agreed over the last few decades to reduce their tariffs.

Many countries, however, still impose high tariffs on certain categories of import, such as textiles. Their aim is less to raise revenue for the government than to protect domestic industries from foreign COMPETITION.

TAX AVOIDANCE
This is the legal practice of making tax bills as small as possible. Tax authorities have no obligation to show taxpayers (be they individuals or corporations) how to pay a minimum amount of tax. On the other hand, no taxpayer is obliged to pay more than the minimum due.

This has led to a huge industry in tax advice. Advisers can make taxpayers aware of tax allowances that are only available if actually claimed. They can also advise on ways of channelling income from different parts of the world into "tax havens": countries or bits of countries with low tax rates and (usually) little else.

The whole tax-avoidance business is unproductive, and adds not one jot nor tittle to the wealth of nations. Ideally it too should be avoided by the imposition of simple-to-collect and simple-to-calculate taxes (like VAT) instead of complicated things like corporation tax, a tax which raises very little revenue for considerable cost.

TAX EVASION
The illegal practice of not paying taxes by making false declarations of income or CAPITAL.

TEST MARKETING
The launch of a new product on to a restricted MARKET to test the public's response before incurring the full COST of launching nationally or internationally. For CONSUMER goods, test marketing is often done in regions covered by a single commercial television station.

THEORIES X AND Y
Two opposing views of human nature (and of the ways to manage a workforce) described by a psychologist, Douglas McGregor, in the late 1950s. Theory X assumes that human beings are lazy and want to avoid work; they have to be coerced and cajoled into working.

Theory Y assumes that people quite naturally find work satisfying, and that they are therefore best left alone to complete tasks.

TIME AND MOTION
A system for measuring the speed and efficiency at which a worker operates in order both to improve them and to set standards for other workers to meet.

Time and motion "studies" are now out of fashion, belonging to an industrial age when the distinction between men and machines was less well appreciated.

TIME MANAGEMENT
The way in which individual managers organise

the use of their own time; a favourite subject for checklists. Here is one.

❏ Plan each day the night before.
❏ Make a list of tasks in order of priority, and work out the time needed for each.
❏ Isolate the key tasks and make sure that they get done.
❏ Do not clutter the day with tasks that can wait.
❏ Build in time for solitude, or for an unpredictable problem that could arise.
❏ Reduce interruptions from phone calls and so on at times earmarked for tasks.
❏ Relate each day to the rest of the week, month, and so on, and to your goals.

TIME SHEET
A card on which is kept a record of the hours worked by employees each day, in order to calculate their weekly wages. The wages will normally be based on a certain minimum number of working hours, anything above them being paid at OVERTIME rates.

TOTAL QUALITY MANAGEMENT
A MANAGEMENT idea that spread rapidly from Japan to the USA and Europe. Often referred to as TQM, it maintains that it is not enough for a corporation to leave QUALITY CONTROL as a final check at the end of a production line. Quality must infuse the organisation and everything about the production process, from the very beginning to the end. Only that way can quality products and services be guaranteed.

Confusingly, quality is a word that means different things to different people.

One survey of top managers came up with the following definitions, in descending order of popularity.

• Better than the COMPETITION; stands out from the rest.
• VALUE for money; COST-effectiveness.

- Reliability; consistency; delivery on time.
- Efficiency; does the job intended.
- Meets the needs of the customer.
- Exceeds the expectations of the customer.
- DESIGN; appearance is good.
- Speed of response; swift resolution of problems.

TRADEMARK

The special mark that a manufacturer puts on its products to distinguish them from other manufacturers' products. For example, the camel on a packet of cigarettes.

Trademarks can be registered so that nobody else can use them legally without permission. Nevertheless, they are frequently stolen by counterfeiters. Yves St Laurent reckons it loses $60m a year from sales of fake bottles of its perfume.

TRADE UNIONS

Organisations formed by a group of workers who get together to use the power of COLLECTIVE BARGAINING to improve their lot. Workers pay a fee to the union to become members, and the union then negotiates pay and conditions with employers on their behalf. Unions organise strikes and support their members while they are on strike (and unpaid).

Many unions are organised according to the craft of their members (electricians, stevedores, and so on), but some are organised by industry (banking, coal-mining, and so on) and some consist only of the employees of a single firm. In such cases they are usually referred to as staff associations. There are country variations.

Trade could not be managed by those who manage it if it had so much difficulty.
Samuel Johnson

TRAINING

Teaching employees new knowledge or skills in order that they can do their current jobs better, or so that they can move to other jobs within the same organisation.

Companies set about training employees in many different ways. The very biggest have their own training centres where staff are sent from time to time. The accountancy and management consultancy firm Arthur Andersen has a vast training centre near Chicago which is almost like an in-house university for all Andersen's employees around the world. It has a research centre and acts as the guardian of Andersen's CORPORATE CULTURE. Big high-tech companies like Boeing and IBM spend up to 3.5% of their total sales on training.

Some companies bring in specialist trainers to teach particular skills, but rely on in-house trainers for the rest of the time. Others send employees to professional trainers' courses, or sponsor them on formal education programmes like the MBA. Yet other companies give employees no training whatsoever.

TRANSFER PRICING

The practice of shifting a PROFIT from one country (with a high tax rate) to another (with a low tax rate); transfer pricing skirts on the boundary between TAX AVOIDANCE and TAX EVASION.

Before governments clamped down on transfer pricing it was popular with multinationals. One SUBSIDIARY (in country A) would charge another subsidiary (in country B) a higher-than-market price for an intra-group purchase of goods or services. That would make no difference to the multinational's overall profit, but it would shift more of it to country B and less to country A, which is nice if country B has a lower corporation tax rate than country A.

TROUBLESHOOTER

Sometimes known as an "interim manager". A person sent into a COMPANY for a short period to sort out a particular problem. Troubleshooters are valued for the "fresh eye" that they can bring. Unlike management consultants, they have a remit to do something about problems that they identify.

One description of an ideal troubleshooter from a firm that supplies them is as follows.

A troubleshooter, or crisis manager, is typically aged 40 or older, has at least ten years of board-level management experience and is able to gain a rapid insight into how a business works at all levels and across all functions, such as marketing, production and finance. He or she also needs to be a good communicator, creative and flexible, as well as mentally and physically tough enough to cope with the stresses of rescuing a company.

The firm which wrote this job description says it receives 2,000 applications from potential trouble-shooters every year, but accepts fewer than 1% of them. It is amazing that it finds so many.

TURNKEY PROJECT

A large-scale project (such as the building of a new FACTORY or ship) where the contractor agrees to see to every single detail of the construction; the buyer only has to "turn the key" when the project is handed over to it.

TURNOVER

The VALUE of all goods sold by an organisation within a period (less goods returned). Turnover is also called sales. It is a key figure because:

• stockbrokers and their analysts want to compare it with last year's figure and generally turn it inside out;
• the tax inspector sometimes wants to base a tax on it, known as a turnover or sales tax;
• competitors want to know whether they are increasing their MARKET share.

U

UNDERCAPITALISED

The common situation of a COMPANY which has too little CAPITAL for the amount of business that it is doing, or that it is setting out to do. (See also OVERTRADING.)

UNIQUE SELLING PROPOSITION

Once upon a time all good MARKETING people would say "Woe betide the new product that is without a USP." A unique selling proposition (USP) was to a product what "star quality" was to a Hollywood hopeful: absolutely necessary for success, but not sufficient.

A product's USP is the range of unique features that differentiate it from its competitors and that can be conveyed to consumers in a simple ADVERTISING message. Marketing people, however, soon discovered that uniqueness is a rare quality, and that it is too much to hope to find it in every new product. So uniqueness gave way to comparison: differentiation from its competitors according to the product's position on a scale of qualities.

UPMARKET

A MARKETING term describing the higher-price end of the spectrum of a market: Bond Street, not Oxford Street; Fifth Avenue, not SoHo. Whether to move upmarket is an important strategic issue for many companies. Should they continue to sell low-price, low VALUE-added goods where COMPETITION is increasingly fierce; or should they change to higher-value goods, selling less of them but making more PROFIT on each unit sold? In fashion, food and electronics, companies move upmarket almost constantly.

In a few instances companies decide on the opposite strategy. The Pierre Cardin business, for example, was once a high-fashion French label. Then it decided to stick its name on to all sorts of "popular" DOWNMARKET products with considerable success.

USER-FRIENDLY

A term applied to computers that are easy to use,

or that provide their user with clear instructions. Early generations of computers were so complex that they could only be operated by boffins with a PhD. Nowadays manufacturers aim to make their machines accessible to all.

USP
See UNIQUE SELLING PROPOSITION.

V

VALUE

As in "He is a man who knows the price of everything and the value of nothing." Value is a subjective measure of worth: what something is worth to its owner. That may be more than the price tag says it cost (as, say, in the case of jewellery received on special occasions); or it may be less (as in the case of the "free" airline ticket that demands the traveller stay in a particular expensive hotel on arrival).

MARKETING can be described as the art of making consumers feel that they have at least got "value for money"; that is, the product (and all its associations) is worth to them at least as much as they paid for it.

VALUE-ADDED TAX

A simple-to-collect tax imposed on consumption. Popular in Europe, value-added tax (VAT) is imposed at every stage of the production process. It is paid by the purchaser of goods and services, and is levied as a percentage of the selling price. Manufacturers pay VAT on their input and then charge VAT on their sales. They hand over to the revenue the tax that they have collected, net of the tax that they have paid. So the revenue ends up, in effect, collecting tax on the VALUE added at each stage of the manufacturing process. Yet the burden of paying the tax actually falls on the final CONSUMER.

Different rates of VAT apply to different goods and services. Some things, like books and children's clothes, may be "zero-rated" (that is there is no VAT on them at all). Within the EUROPEAN COMMUNITY strenuous efforts are being made to harmonise rates of VAT, and what is or is not zero-rated.

VALUE CHAIN

The interlinking activities carried out within a corporation. Identifying those activities and learning how to perform them more cheaply or better than competitors is the way for a COMPANY to gain competitive advantage, according to Michael

Porter in *Competitive Advantage: Sustaining Superior Performance* (Free Press, 1985).

VAT

See VALUE-ADDED TAX.

VISION

Something beyond optical perception that enables one manager to anticipate and avoid commercial disaster while another (without it) trips and falls. Vision is built on imagination, and imagination is in short supply in business life.

VORSTAND

The MANAGEMENT BOARD in Germany's system of two-tier boards (see *AUFSICHTSRAT*). Members of the *Vorstand* cannot be members of the *Aufsichtsrat*, and vice versa. *Vorstand* members are appointed for fixed terms of office, and deal with the day-to-day management of the COMPANY.

W

WAGE FREEZE
The halting by government of increases in wages in order to control INFLATION. This is done in the belief that wages and prices are so closely linked that freezing one must have a similar effect on the other. While wage freezes may slow down the pace of wage increases they never freeze them altogether, if only because there are always a large number of exceptions, and an equally large number of loopholes.

WASTING ASSET
The type of ASSET that is exhausted over time (excluding those that are merely exhausted by a long lunch). Such assets include:

• mines that will eventually run out of whatever is being extracted from them;
• the fleet of company cars that will in time be good only for the scrapheap; and
• the machine that will one day cost more to repair than to replace.

WHITE-COLLAR WORKER
A person who arrives at work with a white collar and its standard accompaniment, the tie. Why has such an uncomfortable combination become the standard uniform of MANAGEMENT (except in a few progressive companies like Levi Strauss)? (See BLUE-COLLAR WORKER.)

WHITE GOODS
Originally white household goods like sheets and towels. The expression has been taken over by MARKETING people to refer more specifically to white electrical household goods, such as refrigerators and washing machines. To be contrasted with BROWN GOODS.

Manufacturers which make white goods tend to diversify into manufacturing other white goods, and likewise for brown goods. It is rare to find the same COMPANY making both white and brown goods, although the Dutch firm Philips is one exception.

W

WINDING-UP
See LIQUIDATION.

WINDOW-DRESSING
The use of various accounting techniques to make a COMPANY's annual ACCOUNTS (its "window" on the world) look as appealing as possible. The techniques in question are usually legal, so window-dressing is a more subtle process than a simple cooking of the books.

For the PROFIT AND LOSS ACCOUNT, window-dressing techniques boil down to two.

* **Accelerating revenues.**
* **Postponing expenses.**

Techniques for the balance sheet also boil down to two.

* **Overvaluing ASSETS.**
* **Undervaluing LIABILITIES.**

The room for judgment in deciding the VALUE of stocks (see LIFO and FIFO), and in deciding whether debts are likely to be repaid or not, provides plenty of opportunities.

WIP
See WORK-IN-PROGRESS.

WITHHOLDING TAX
Tax that is withheld at source and paid directly to the revenue without ever passing through a taxpayer's hands. Income tax is withheld at source by many employers from wages and salaries. Tax on interest and DIVIDEND income is often withheld by financial institutions, especially on payments to non-residents. OFFSHORE financial centres thrive on serving people who do not want their tax thus withheld.

WORK-IN-PROGRESS
Referred to in the USA as work-in-process, this includes all the semi-finished goods and services

in a business, things on their way from being RAW MATERIALS and supplies to becoming finished products. Firms try to reduce expensive work-in-progress (WIP) to a minimum. By introducing JIT systems at one factory, Hewlett Packard cut its WIP from 22 days' worth to one day's worth.

For many companies (like contractors) almost all their ASSETS consist of work-in-process, so valuing this unfinished business is very significant in any estimation of such a company's worth. But how can you VALUE things like a half-built hotel in Harare?

WORK-TO-RULE
A technique used by workers in industrial disputes. They refuse to do any OVERTIME; stick rigidly to the COMPANY's rule book; and generally waste time.

WORKER PARTICIPATION
A practice common in continental Europe, but which Anglo-Saxon companies seem to find philosophically objectionable and fit only for near-communists. Worker participation involves employees in some or all of the following:

• being allowed and encouraged to own shares in the company they work for;
• having representation on the BOARD;
• having access, as a right, to information about their company;
• having some CONTROL over the MANAGEMENT of their own pension fund;
• having access to exactly the same facilities – car parks, toilets, and so on – as so-called management.

Worker participation is an attempt to bridge the gap between the white-collar manager and the BLUE-COLLAR WORKER. In Japan it is as much a way of life as *sushi*; and the Japanese have never been communists.

I'm not going to have the monkeys running the zoo.

Frank Borman, when chairman of Eastern Airlines, expressing his attitude to worker participation. Monkeys may have done a better job; Eastern went bust.

WORKING CAPITAL

The difference between a COMPANY's current ASSETS and its current LIABILITIES; that is, the amount of cash it has free and available to run the business. Current assets include easily sellable goods, cash and bank deposits; current liabilities include debts due in less than a year, interest payments, and so on. The classic solution to a shortage of working capital is a visit to the bank.

WORKSTATION

A configuration of computers that stands alone on an individual's desk and can complete required tasks (such as word processing, spreadsheet work, and so on) without access to a NETWORK.

WRONGFUL DISMISSAL

Sacking an employee for a reason that is not sufficient to justify such extreme action. The law protects employees against what was once common practice. If wrongful dismissal can be proved in the courts the victim has a right to compensation. From the idea of wrongful dismissal has come the concept of "constructive dismissal". In this case an employee is treated by an employer in such a way (unjustifiably demoted or victimised without actually being sacked) that he or she has the right to resign and claim wrongful dismissal.

YIELD

In general this refers to the output of any of the factors of production (land, LABOUR and CAPITAL). Thus yield can refer to the wheat produced per year per acre from a particular plot of land, or it can refer to the tonnes of coal dug up by a single miner in a year.

It is most commonly used with reference to the annual return (the output) from an investment of capital. An investment of $1,000 that produces $90 in a year has a yield of 9%. This sort of yield comes in several forms.

• **DIVIDEND yield.** The annual pre-tax amount that shareholders receive as dividend, expressed as a percentage of the amount they invested.
• **Earnings yield.** The pre-tax profits of a COMPANY (its "earnings") divided by the number of shares, expressed as a percentage of the price per SHARE. This is the reciprocal of the P/E RATIO.
• **Flat yield.** The yield taking into account only the income earned on an investment; the sort of yield obtained from a bank deposit where the capital sum does not change from the moment it is made to the time it is withdrawn.
• **Gross/net yield.** The yield expressed before/after tax is paid.
• **Redemption yield.** A yield which takes into account any capital gain (or loss) to be made on the redemption of an investment. This is particularly useful in calculating the return to be made on fixed-interest SECURITIES (like government bonds). These are issued with a fixed rate of interest and then sold in the secondary MARKET at a DISCOUNT or at a premium to their "redemption price", depending on whether current market rates are higher or lower than their fixed rate.

ZAIBATSU

The large groups of Japanese financial and industrial companies that are interlinked by cross-shareholdings and long-term commercial links. Such groups include Mitsubishi, Sumitomo and Mitsui. A more modern name for these groups is "*keiretsu*", which means "headless combines".

Many have attributed Japan's industrial success to the existence of the *zaibatsu*, but others argue that the fastest-growing Japanese companies of the past two decades have been firms like Toyota, Sony and Canon, none of them part of a *zaibatsu*.

ZERO-BASE BUDGETING

A popular way of drawing up budgets which assumes that there was no budget at all last year. Managers are asked to justify all expenditure afresh each year. They are not allowed to get away with justifying only the increase. In practice, zero-base budgeting (ZBB) is time-consuming and difficult to implement, but the idea that no expenditure should ever be taken for granted is a healthy one.

ZERO DEFECT

Some Japanese companies have the audacious ambition to produce goods that have no faults whatsoever. Few if any achieve it; but if none of them had the ambition, then for sure none of them would achieve it.

My work is done, why wait?
Suicide note of the 78 year-old George Eastman, founder of Eastman Kodak

---

Part 3

APPENDIXES

Part 3

APPENDICES

Table 1 The UK's most admired companies

Rank	Company
1	Glaxo
2	Unilever
3	Rentokil
4	Guinness
5	Reuters
6	Marks & Spencer
7	Shell
8	J. Sainsbury
9	SmithKline Beecham
10	Redland
11	Wellcome
12	Central Independent TV
13	Body Shop
14	Cadbury Schweppes
15	Allied Colloids
16	RTZ
17	Yorkshire Electricity
18	Reckitt & Colman
19	Tesco
20	BOC

Source: The Economist,
October 17th 1992

Table 2 The USA's most admired companies

Rank	Company
1	Merck
2	Rubbermaid
3	Wal-Mart Stores
4	3M
5	Coca-Cola
6	Procter & Gamble
7	Levi Strauss Associates
8	Liz Claiborne
9	J. P. Morgan
10	Boeing

Source: Fortune, February 8th 1993, from a poll of over 8,000 executives

Table 3 The world's most productive industrial companies, quoted on a recognised stock exchange, 1992

Highest in sales per employee	Sales rank	$
Idemitsu Kosan	83	3,004,008
Cosmo Oil	126	2,866,512
Shara Shell Sekiyu	134	2,704,572
Nintendo	289	2,093,735
Lyondell Petrochemical	311	2,082,612
Seiko	456	2,042,084
Mitsubishi Oil	211	2,034,158
Honam Oil Refinery	357	1,862,526
Nippon Oil	62	1,798,606
General Sekiyu	450	1,797,722

Highest in sales/$ of stockholders' equity		
Kanebo	284	122.46
Taiyo Fishery	187	40.89
Entreprise Minière & Chimique	466	38.29
Idemitsu Kosan	83	30.34
Ferruzzi Finanziarta	75	23.92
Isuzu Motors	110	21.75
General Motors	1	21.33
IBP	127	20.84
FMC	360	18.23
Outokumpu	416	18.14

Source: Fortune, July 26th 1993

Table 4 The world's most profitable industrial companies, quoted on a recognised stock exchange, 1992

Highest returns on assets	Sales rank	%
Astra	474	21.4
American Home Products	191	20.5
General Dynamics	168	19.3
Bristol-Myers Squibb	121	18.2
Merck	142	17.9
Abbott Laboratories	189	17.9
Schering-Plough	353	17.3
SmithKline Beecham	150	17.0
Glaxo Holdings	201	16.8
SCA	270	16.3
The 500 Median		1.8
Highest returns on assets		
Astra	474	21.4
American Home Products	191	20.5
General Dynamics	168	19.3
Bristol-Myers Squibb	121	18.2
Merck	142	17.9
Abbott Laboratories	189	17.9
Schering-Plough	353	17.3
SmithKline Beecham	150	17.0
Glaxo Holdings	201	16.8
SCA	270	16.3
The 500 Median		1.8
Highest returns on sales		
Glaxo	201	24.2
Petronas	226	23.7
Astra	474	20.8
De Beers Consolidated Mines	392	20.7
Merck	142	20.2
SCA	270	19.0
American Home Products	191	18.6
Intel	254	17.8
Schering-Plough	353	17.6
Bristol-Myers Squibb	12.1	16.6
The 500 Median		1.7

Source: Fortune, July 26th 1993

Table 5 The world's biggest companies by industry, 1992

Industry	Company	Country	Sales ($m)
Aerospace	Boeing	USA	30,414
Apparel	Levi Strauss Associates	USA	5,570
Beverages	PepsiCo	USA	22,084
Building materials	Saint-Gobain	France	14,297
Chemicals	E.I. du Pont de Nemours	USA	37,386
Computers[a]	IBM	USA	65,096
Electronics	General Electric	USA	62,202
Food	Philip Morris	USA	50,157
Forest products	International Paper	USA	13,600
Industrial & farm equipment	Mitsubishi Heavy Industries	Japan	23,011
Jewellery, silverware	Citizen Watch	Japan	3,328
Metal products	Pechiney	France	12,344
Metals	IRI	Italy	67,547
Mining, crude oil production	Ruhrkohle	Germany	15,712
Motor vehicles & parts	General Motors	USA	132,775
Petroleum refining	Exxon	USA	103,547
Pharmaceuticals	Johnson & Johnson	USA	13,846
Publishing, printing	Matra-Hachette	France	10,416
Rubber & plastics products	Bridgestone	Japan	13,860
Scientific & photographic equipment	Eastman Kodak	USA	20,577
Soaps, cosmetics	Procter & Gamble	USA	29,890
Textiles	Toray Industries	Japan	7,862
Tobacco	RJR Nabisco	USA	15,734
Toys, sporting goods	Nintendo	Japan	5,213
Transportation equipment	Hyundai Heavy Industries	S. Korea	6,518

[a] Including office equipment.

Source: Fortune, July 26th 1993

Table 6 Comparative corporate tax survey

Country	Top corporate tax rates[a] (%) July, 1993
Austria	39.0
Belgium	40.2
Denmark	34.0
Finland	25.0
France	33.3
Germany	59.7 on retained profits
	48.4 on distributed profits
Greece	35.0
Ireland	40
	10 for manufacturing and many service companies[b]
Italy	52.2
Netherlands	40 for taxable profits up to Dfl250,000
	35 for profits above that
Norway	28
Portugal	39.9
Spain	35.0
Sweden	30.0
Switzerland	28.5
UK	33
	25 for companies with profits up to £250,000

[a] Including local taxes, where applicable.
[b] Applies for manufacturing companies up to 2010, and for companies trading services internationally from Dublin Customs Docks Area up to 2005.

Source: KPMG

Table 7 EC statutory retirement age

Country	Men	Women
Denmark	67	67
Belgium	65	60
Germany	65	65
Greece	65	60
Ireland	65	65
Luxembourg	65	65
Netherlands	65	65
Portugal	65	60
Spain	65	65
UK	65	60
France	60	60
Italy	60	55

Source: Eurostat, 1991

Table 8 EC[a] public spending on R&D, 1990

Country	% of GDP
Germany[b]	2.8
France	2.4
UK	2.3
Netherlands	2.2
Belgium	1.6
Denmark	1.5
Italy	1.4
Spain	0.9
Ireland	0.8
Portugal	0.5
Greece	0.5

[a] Excluding Luxembourg.
[b] West Germany only.

Source: OECD, Main Science and Technology Indicators, 1992

Table 9 The most expensive cities in the world

Rank	City	Index (New York = 100)
1	Tokyo	198
2	Osaka Kobe	180
3	Libreville	143
4	Tripoli	142
5	Brazzaville	137
6	Abidjan	135
7	Oslo	132
8	Paris	124
9	Zurich	122
10	Dakar	120
	Taipei	120
12	Vienna	119
13	Douala	117
14	Copenhagen	115
15	Geneva	113
16	Seoul	112
17	Munich	108
	Stockholm	108
19	Frankfurt	107
	Brussels	107
	Hong Kong	107

Source: Business International, *Cost of Living Survey*, March 1993

Table 11 EC average weekly working hours, 1991

Country	Hours per week
UK	43.4
Portugal	41.5
Spain	40.5
Ireland	40.5
Greece	40.3
Luxembourg	39.9
Germany	39.8
France	39.7
Netherlands	39.0
Italy	38.6
Denmark	38.4
Belgium	37.9
EC average	38.9

Source: Eurostat, 1993

Table 10 Relative salaries around the world in terms of purchasing power (London=100; spring 1991)

	Production department head	Secretary
New York	260	134
Dusseldorf	186	131
Toronto	184	119
Vienna	151	120
Paris	147	97
Geneva	146	153
Tokyo	137	88
Brussels	136	101
Hong Kong	129	94
Amsterdam	127	123
Singapore	114	68
Sydney	112	119
Dublin	111	90
Copenhagen	100	104
London	100	100
Helsinki	91	80
Milan	91	93
Madrid	71	105
Stockholm	58	62
Lisbon	57	52
Oslo	46	71

Source: Union Bank of Switzerland

Table 12 EC average days paid vacation

Country	Normal paid vacation[a]	Statutory entitlement	Public holidays
Germany	40	18	10
Belgium	39	20	11
Spain	38	25	10
France	37	25	8
Sweden	36	27	11
Denmark	35	25	10
Greece	35	24	9
Portugal	35	21	9
Italy	34	–	8
Switzerland	33	20	11
Netherlands	33	20	8
UK	31	–	8
Ireland	28	15	8

[a] Including public holidays.

Source: EC Commission, DG XI

Table 13 Comparative labour costs in manufacturing, 1992
(Average hourly compensation, including non-wage costs, in $ and local currencies)

Country	$[a]	Local currency[b]
Europe (high)		
Germany	25.94	40.51
Sweden	24.23	141.14
Switzerland	23.26	32.70
Norway	23.20	144.17
Belgium	22.01	707.77
Netherlands	20.72	36.44
Denmark	20.02	120.88
Austria	19.65	215.91
Europe (medium)		
Italy	19.41	23,909
Finland	18.69	83.87
France	16.88	89.37
UK	14.69	8.32
Spain	13.39	1,371
Ireland	13.32	7.81
Europe (low)		
Greece	7.04	1,342
Portugal	5.01	673.73
Non-Europe		
USA	16.17	–
Japan	16.16	–

[a] Average annual exchange rate.
[b] Appropriate national currency.

Source: US Bureau of Labor Statistics; Business International, *Business Europe*, September 6th 1993

Table 14 Top 50 of the *Fortune Global 500*

COMPANY	COUNTRY	SALES $bn	SALES % change from 1991	PROFITS $bn	PROFITS Rank	PROFITS % change from 1991	ASSETS $bn	ASSETS Rank	STOCK HOLDERS' EQUITY $bn	STOCK HOLDERS' EQUITY Rank	EMPLOYEES No.	EMPLOYEES Rank
General Motors	USA	132.77	7.3	−23.50	500	–	191.01	2	6.23	68	750,000	1
Exxon	USA	103.55	0.3	4.77	3	−14.8	85.03	6	33.78	4	95,000	67
Ford Motor	USA	100.79	13.3	−7.39	494	–	180.55	3	14.75	14	325,333	7
Royal Dutch/Shell Group	UK/Netherlands	98.94	−4.7	5.40	1	27.3	100.35	4	52.94	1	127,000	41
Toyota Motor	Japan	79.11	1.3	1.81	12	−42.4	76.13	8	37.49	2	108,167	54
IRI	Italy	67.55	5.4	−3.81	491	–	n.a.		n.a.		400,000	3
IBM	USA	65.10	−0.5	−4.97	493	–	86.71	5	27.62	6	308,010	8
Daimler-Benz	Germany	63.34	10.5	0.93	36	−17.8	53.21	13	11.42	24	376,467	4
General Electric	USA	62.20	3.3	4.73	4	79.2	192.88	1	23.46	8	268,000	12
Hitachi	Japan	61.47	3.1	0.62	59	−35.4	76.67	7	25.77	7	331,505	6
British Petroleum	UK	59.22	1.5	−0.81	476	−200.7	52.64	14	15.10	12	97,650	64
Matsushita Electric Industrial	Japan	57.48	0.5	0.31	124	−69.1	75.65	9	30.06	5	252,075	14
Mobil	USA	57.39	0.8	0.86	40	−55.1	40.56	24	16.54	10	63,700	100
Volkswagen	Germany	56.73	23.2	0.05	306	−92.5	46.48	20	8.36	43	274,103	11

COMPANY	COUNTRY	SALES		PROFITS			ASSETS		STOCK HOLDERS' EQUITY		EMPLOYEES	
		$bn	% change from 1991	$bn	Rank	% change from 1991	$bn	Rank	$bn	Rank	No.	Rank
Siemens	Germany	51.40	14.6	1.14	25	0.1	50.75	15	13.51	16	413,000	2
Nissan Motor	Japan	50.25	2.8	0.45	460	-159.0	62.98	10	15.09	13	143,754	31
Philip Morris	USA	50.16	4.3	4.94	2	64.3	50.01	16	12.56	18	161,000	25
Samsung	South Korea	49.56	11.5	0.37	105	7.7	48.03	19	6.43	66	188,588	19
Fiat	Italy	47.93	2.4	0.45	84	-50.3	58.01	11	11.61	23	285,482	9
Unilever	UK/Netherlands	43.96	6.5	2.28	5	11.8	24.27	49	6.93	57	283,000	10
ENI	Italy	40.37	-1.7	-0.77	473	-188.0	54.79	12	11.01	25	124,032	46
Elf Aquitaine	France	39.72	7.0	1.17	23	-32.9	45.13	21	15.74	11	87,900	74
Nestlé	Switzerland	39.06	9.8	1.92	9	11.3	30.34	39	8.89	40	218,005	15
Chevron	USA	38.52	4.7	1.57	15	21.3	33.97	34	13.73	15	49,245	143
Toshiba	Japan	37.47	5.7	0.16	200	-44.5	49.34	18	10.07	29	173,000	22
E. I. du Pont de Nemours	USA	37.39	-2.5	-3.93	492	-379.9	38.87	29	11.77	22	125,000	43
Texaco	USA	37.13	-1.1	0.71	48	-45.0	25.99	44	9.97	30	37,582	199
Chrysler	USA	36.90	25.6	0.72	46	–	40.65	23	7.54	48	128,000	39
Renault	France	33.88	15.1	1.07	28	96.5	23.90	54	6.15	70	146,604	29
Honda Motor	Japan	33.37	0.9	0.31	125	-37.0	26.37	43	9.09	35	90,900	69
Philips Electronics	Netherlands	33.27	10.1	-0.51	465	-179.6	26.85	42	4.99	90	252,200	13

Company	Country											
Sony	Japan	31.45	7.9	0.29	133	-67.8	39.70	25	12.52	19	126,000	42
ABB ASEA Brown Boveri	Switzerland	30.54	2.8	0.51	73	-17.1	25.95	45	4.10	113	213,407	16
Alcatel Alsthom	France	30.53	7.5	1.33	18	21.5	44.21	22	9.03	37	203,000	17
Boeing	USA	30.41	2.8	0.55	66	-64.8	18.15	73	8.06	46	143,000	32
Procter & Gamble	USA	29.89	9.1	1.87	10	5.6	24.03	53	9.07	36	106,200	57
Hoechst	Germany	29.57	3.0	0.59	63	-10.6	22.79	58	7.31	52	177,668	21
Peugeot	France	29.39	3.5	0.64	57	-35.0	23.35	56	9.62	32	150,800	27
BASF	Germany	28.49	1.3	0.39	98	-37.3	24.06	52	8.95	38	123,254	47
NEC	Japan	28.38	-0.8	-0.36	453	-415.5	34.87	32	7.06	56	140,969	33
Daewoo	South Korea	28.33	11.7	0.38	102	–	39.25	27	5.13	86	78,727	83
Fujitsu	Japan	27.91	7.1	-0.26	436	-385.0	33.09	36	9.65	31	161,974	24
Bayer	Germany	26.63	2.9	0.97	34	-11.8	23.66	55	10.54	27	156,400	26
Mitsubishi Electric	Japan	26.50	3.7	0.23	159	-15.7	30.75	38	7.15	54	107,859	55
Total	France	26.14	1.5	0.54	69	-47.8	20.92	61	7.38	51	51,139	137
Amoco	USA	25.54	-0.2	-0.07	390	-105.0	28.45	41	12.96	17	46,994	155
Mitsubishi Motors	Japan	25.48	8.2	0.21	169	-6.6	20.94	60	3.52	137	45,000	164
Nippon Steel	Japan	23.99	-2.5	0.01	356	-97.5	39.22	28	9.16	34	51,900	133
Mitsubishi Heavy Industries	Japan	23.01	7.1	0.65	54	-18.1	35.35	31	9.34	33	66,000	96
Thyssen	Germany	22.73	0.6	0.21	168	-29.3	16.65	88	3.42	140	147,279	28

GLOSSARY

French

Achats Purchases
Actif/passif Assets/liabilities
Action Share (stock)
Actionnaire Shareholder
Amortissement Depreciation
Assemblée générale General meeting
Association Partnership
Associé Partner
Autorisation d'exporter Export licence
Bilan Balance sheet
Bourse Stock exchange
Brut/net Gross/net
Bureau Office
CAF Cif
Cedex Postal sorting office
Chiffre d'affaires Turnover/sales
Comptable Accountant
Comptes Accounts
Compte de pertes et profits Profit and loss account
Conseil d'administration Board of directors
Concurrence Competition
Contingent d'importation Import quota
Créancier Creditor
Débiteur Debtor
Devises Foreign exchange
Emprunt Loan
Fabrique/usine Factory
Facture Invoice
Faillite Bankrupt
Filiale Subsidiary
Le fisc Inland Revenue
Flux de liquidités Cash flow
Fonds de roulement Capital/working capital
Fonds propres Own funds/shareholders' equity
Frais Costs
Frais généraux Overheads
Fusion Merger
Gérant Manager
Gestion Management
Gros Wholesale
Heures supplémentaires Overtime
Homme d'affaires Businessman
Hors taxes Duty-free
Impôts Taxes/duties
Inventaire Inventory/stock
Marchandises Goods
Marché Market
Marché Commun Common Market/EC
Marque Brand
Matières premières Raw materials
Obligation Bond
PDG (président directeur général) Executive chairman
Perte Loss
PME (petites et moyennes entreprises) Small and medium-sized businesses
Portefeuille Portfolio
Prêt Loan
Prime Premium
Prix d'achat Purchase price
Propriétaire Owner
Recherche industrielle R&D
Réclame Advertisement
Recrutement recruitment
Réunion Meeting
Sécurités Securities
Siège social Head office
SMIC (salaire minimum interprofessionel de croissance) Minimum wage
Société Company
Société anonyme (SA) Limited company
Société en commandite Limited partnership
Solvabilité (degré de solvabilité) Credit rating
Succursale Branch
Syndicat Trade union

Titres Securities
TVA (taxe à la valeur ajoutée) VAT

German

Aktie Share
Aktiengesellschaft (AG) Public
  company
Aktiva/Passiva
  Assets/liabilities
Arbeit Work
Aufsichtsrat Supervisory board
Ausführgenehmigung Export
  licence
Betriebskapital Working
  capital
Börse Stock exchange
Brutto/netto Gross/net
Buchhalter Accountant
Büro Office
Cash-flow Cash flow
Devisen Foreign exchange
Einführkontingent Import
  quota
Einstellung Recruitment
Fabrik Factory
Filiale Associate
Finanzamt Inland Revenue
Generalunkosten Overheads
Geschäft Business
Gesellschaft Company
*Gesellschaft mit beschränkter
  Haftung (GmbH)* Limited
  liability company
Gewerkschaft Trade union
Gläubiger Creditor
Haben Credit
Handel Trade
Handelskammer Chamber of
  commerce
Handelsvertreter Commercial
  agent
Hauptbüro Head office
Hauptversammlung
  Shareholders' meeting
Inventar Inventory/stock
Kapital Capital
Kasse Cash desk
Kaufmann Businessman
KG (Kommanditgesellschaft)
Limited partnership
Kombinate East German
  conglomerate
Konkurrenz Competition
Konkurs Bankruptcy
Konto Accounts
Körperschaftsteuer
  Corporation tax
Kredietwürdigkeit Credit rating
Lager Warehouse
Landesbank Regional bank
Marke Brand
Mehrwertsteuer VAT
Messe Trade fair
Muster Sample
Niederlassung Branch
*Offene Handelsgesellschaft
  (OHG)* General partnership
Rechnung Invoice
Rechnungsabschluss Balance
  sheet
Saldo Balance
Schaden Damage
Schuldner Debtor
Sicherheit Securities
Spesen Expenses
Treffen Meeting
Überstunden Overtime
Umsatz Turnover/sales
Unternehmen Firm/company
Verboten Forbidden
Versicherung Insurance
Vorstand Board of directors
Wechselkurs Exchange rate
Werbung Publicity
Wert Value
Wirtschaftsprüfer Qualified
  accountant
Zins Interest
Zoll Customs
*Zweckforschung; Forschung
  und Entwicklung* R&D
Zwischenhändler Middleman

RECOMMENDED READING LIST

James Abegglen and George Stalk, *Kaisha, the Japanese Corporation*, Basic Books, 1985.

C.A. Bartlett and S. Ghoshal, *Managing Across Borders: The Transnational Solution*, Harvard Business School Press, 1989.

J. Constable and R. McCormick, *The Making of British Managers*, BIM/CBI, 1987.

Peter Drucker, *The Effective Executive*, Harper and Row, 1967.

Charles Handy, *Understanding Organisations*, Penguin, 1976.

Charles Handy, *The Age of Unreason*, Hutchinson, 1989.

Sir John Harvey-Jones, *Making It Happen*, Fontana, 1989.

Lee Iacocca, *Iacocca, an Autobiography*, Bantam Books, 1984.

Rosabeth Moss Kanter, *The Change Masters*, Simon and Schuster, 1983.

Harold J. Leavitt, *Management Psychology*, University of Chicago Press, 1978.

Kenichi Ohmae, *The Borderless World*, Harper Business, 1990.

W. Ouchi, *Theory Z: How American Business Can Meet the Japanese Challenge*, Addison-Wesley, 1981.

C. Northcote Parkinson, *Parkinson's Law or the Pursuit of Progress*, Penguin, 1957.

R.T. Pascale and A.G. Athos, *The Art of Japanese Management*, Simon and Schuster, 1981.

Tom Peters and Robert Waterman, *In Search of Excellence*, Harper and Row, 1982.

Tom Peters, *Thriving on Chaos*, Alfred A. Knopf, 1987.

Michael Porter, *Competitive Advantage*, Free Press, 1985.

Michael Porter, *The Competitive Advantage of Nations*, Macmillan, 1990.

C.K. Prahalad and Y.L. Doz, *The Multinational Mission: Balancing Local Demands and Global Vision*, Free Press, 1987.

Edgar H. Schein, *Organisation, Culture and Leadership*, Jossey Bass, 1985.

E.F. Schumacher, *Small is Beautiful*, Blond and Briggs, 1973.

Alfred Sloan, *My Years with General Motors*, Doubleday, 1954.

George Stalk and Thomas M. Hout, *Competing Against Time*, Free Press, 1990.

Alvin Toffler, *Future Shock*, Bantam, 1970.

R. Townsend, *Up the Organisation*, Michael Joseph, 1970.

Shoshana Zuboff, *In the Age of the Smart Machine*, Basic Books, 1988.